Contents

ABOVE: Peppercorn A1 Pacific no. 60163 heads out of Highley on Wednesday, September 21, 2016, during the Severn Valley Railway's Pacific Power charity day event. ROBIN JONES

RIGHT: *Flying Scotsman* heads the Severn Valley Railway's teak train through Bewdley South Junction on September 23, 2016. DUNCAN LANGTREE

CLASH *of the*
STEAM TITANS

AUTHOR: Robin Jones
PRODUCTION EDITOR: Pauline Hawkins
DESIGN: Sean Phillips, atg-media.com
COVER DESIGN: Holly Munro
REPROGRAPHICS: Jonathan Schofield and Paul Fincham
PUBLISHER: Steve O'Hara
PUBLISHING DIRECTOR: Dan Savage
COMMERCIAL DIRECTOR: Nigel Hole
MARKETING MANAGER: Charlotte Park
cpark@mortons.co.uk

PRINTED BY: William Gibbons And Sons, Wolverhampton

DISTRIBUTION EXECUTIVE: JOHN SHARRATT
tradesales@mortons.co.uk
classicmagazines.co.uk/tradesales

ISBN: 978-1-911276-08-1

PUBLISHED BY: Mortons Media Group Ltd, Media Centre, Morton Way, Horncastle, Lincolnshire, LN9 6JR
Tel: 01507 529529

CREDITS: All pictures marked * are published under a Creative Commons licence. Full details may be obtained at http://creativecommons.org/licences

MORTONS
MEDIA GROUP LTD

Introduction

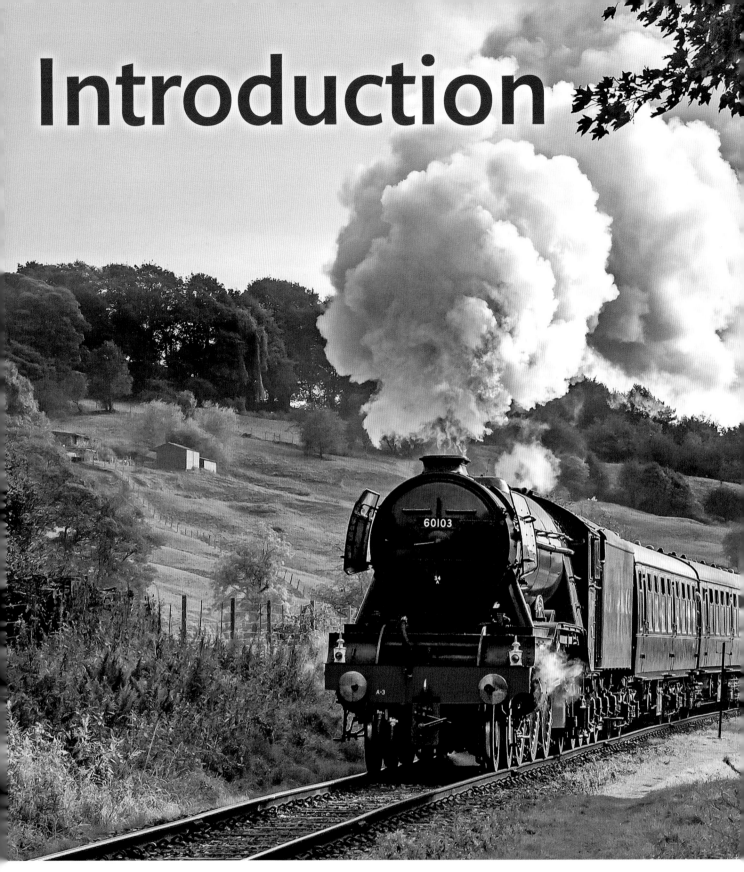

The year 2016 was unique in railway history. For it was the first time that Gresley A3 Pacific No. 60103 (aka 4472) *Flying Scotsman*, the world's most famous locomotive of the 20th century, was running at the same time as its 21st-century counterpart, new-build Peppercorn A1 Pacific No. 60163 *Tornado*.

Flying Scotsman's fame was assured when the LNER publicity machine switched into overdrive in 1924, when it appeared at the British Empire Exhibition at Wembley, and again in 1928 when it hauled the first 'Flying Scotsman' named train nonstop from London to Edinburgh. And it lifted British engineering and transport technology to new dizzy heights in 1934 when it became the first in the world to be officially clocked at 100mph.

And those feats were just for starters.

Since it emerged from Doncaster Works in 1923, *Flying Scotsman* has captured the imagination of people worldwide. It has become a defining icon of the Golden Age of Steam in the 1930s.

There are those who will say "yes, but what about *Mallard* and the 126mph world speed record in 1938?" *Flying Scotsman* never equalled the speed of the legendary A4, but as far as PR was concerned, it had a 14-year head start over No. 4468.

It beggars belief that *Flying Scotsman* so nearly ended up in a scrapyard in 1963, but for the efforts of businessman enthusiast Alan Pegler who bought it. And 41 years later, the perennial crowd-puller finally ended up where it should have been all along – back in public ownership, in the custody of the National Railway Museum.

Flying Scotsman, badly in need of significant repairs, was withdrawn from service at the end of 2005, and spent more than a decade, its longest period out of action in its illustrious history, being rebuilt.

Here, I recall the lines from American singer-songwriter Don McLean's 1972 hit song American Pie:

"Oh and while the king (Elvis Presley) was looking down

LEFT: Gresley A3 Pacific No. 60103 *Flying Scotsman* catches a burst of afternoon sunshine as it powers through Townsend Fold on October 14, 2016, during its second visit of the year to the East Lancashire Railway. ALAN WEAVER

Locomotive Trust again showed Britain in its finest hour, even though the boiler was built in Germany!

And yes, just like the LNER back in 1924, the trust has its own crack publicity machine, essential not only to support the colossal task of fundraising but to ensure growing public support for the ground-breaking project. In both cases, it passes with flying colours.

After it was launched in early 2009, the jester *Tornado* indeed stole the absent A3's thorny crown. From its first main line trip, crowds turned out everywhere to see this gleaming new green celebrity, and even though the novelty of seeing the first steam locomotive built for the British main line since *Evening Star* in 1960 has by now worn off, with *Tornado* part and parcel of the modern heritage charter scene, the crowds have not quite dispersed yet.

However, unprecedented displays of fandom greeted the return of *Flying Scotsman* in January 2016, first in black livery for its test runs on the East Lancashire Railway, and then in BR Brunswick green back where it belongs, on the main line. Admirers have often packed every vantage point along its route, and sadly the T-word – trespass – a negative feature of its previous post-overhaul comeback runs in times past – has resurfaced. Following two incidents where the train and other east coast services were brought to a halt on its official relaunch from King's Cross to York on February 25 followed by others, there have been incidents where train operators have rearranged its trips because of fears that spectators will ignore lineside fences – indeed, in these cases, it has become the locomotive that is too famous to run.

The highlight of 2016, however, was the meeting of both of these steam giants at the Severn Valley Railway's Pacific Power event in September. It is estimated that at least 45,000 people turned out to see the pair in action, even though only a third of that figure were able to obtain tickets to ride, seats having sold out months before. The event, magnificently handled by the line's management and their own superb publicity department, provided a unique platform for the finest of British steam engineering yesterday and today.

We are now in a new golden age of steam, one in which we can look forward to many more adventures involving these steam Titans, both on the national network and on heritage lines. And we look forward to the day when we will be able to see that long-promised line-up of east coast motive power – an A1, A2, A3 and A4. And there are now plans not only to run *Tornado* regularly at its design speed of 90mph, but also to provide it with its own dedicated train.

In building *Tornado*, The A1 Steam Locomotive Trust has laid down blueprints for other new-build projects to follow, and not content to rest on one magnificent achievement, is progressing with others. Its scheme to build the seventh example of an extinct Gresley classic, a P2 2-8-2, No. 2007 *Prince of Wales*, is now the world's fastest-growing standard gauge new-build project, and it now has others in the pipeline.

More great times lie ahead, as exciting new chapters in the history of British steam engineering are written. ●

The jester (Bob Dylan) stole his thorny crown
The courtroom was adjourned
No verdict was returned."

While the King of Steam *Flying Scotsman* encompasses so much that there is to be proud about Britain, during its absence, a jester indeed arose literally out of nowhere, in the form of *Tornado*.

The saving of *Flying Scotsman* meant that the all-conquering A3 class did not pass into extinction. Sadly, the same could not be said for another East Coast Main Line classic, the Peppercorn A1, all 49 of which fell victim to the cutter's torch.

There were those who remembered the class with affection, and decided to do far more than savour wistful memories of glories past. In true 'back of a beermat' style, they hatched a plan to build a new one, not just to run it at 25mph on heritage railways, but on the main line, in regular service. And faced with a mountain range to climb to raise the necessary finance – £3 million – a lack of the steam workshops that regularly turned out locomotives for railway companies and the expertise employed there, and the need to adapt the design to meet the more exacting standards of the main lined network, they succeeded against overwhelming odds. The tenacity, drive and determination, ingenuity and resourcefulness of The A1 Steam

Chapter 1

A flying history of
Flying Scotsman

ABOVE: *Flying Scotsman* complete with LNER cabside crest as it appeared in 1924. By the 1920s, the LNER was marketing the 'Flying Scotsman' service as "The Most Famous Train in the World". ROBIN JONES COLLECTION

On November 30, 2015, the National Railway Museum announced the result of a YouGov survey carried out online across four continents, in which participants were asked to name the most famous locomotive and named train. Respondents in the UK, US, India and Australia were asked to name five trains or locomotives they had heard of.

And there was a clear winner. We in the UK have always known it – but so does the rest of the world, according to the poll. *Flying Scotsman*.

However, other famous steam locomotives that might have topped the railway rankings languished outside the Top Ten Trains table, including the maroon-liveried Hogwarts Express of global Harry Potter fame, which came in at 25th place, while the engine that established railways as the preferred choice of transport and set the blueprint for future steam locomotive development, Stephenson's *Rocket*, came 14th. The Japanese Bullet train, the only example of which outside of Japan is displayed in the York museum's Great Hall, squeezed into 10th position.

LNER A4 Pacific No. 4468, the world's fastest steam locomotive which hit 126mph on Stoke Bank on the East Coast Main Line in Lincolnshire on July 3, 1938, snatching the world record back from Nazi Germany, came in at only eighth.

Museum director Paul Kirkman said: "Our survey, carried out across four global markets, backs up the claim that it is probably the most famous locomotive and express train service in the world." So why is *Flying Scotsman* considered to be the greatest iconic railway locomotive of all time?

I do not propose here to enter into a detailed history of this fabulous steam machine that has been an inspiration for many generations, and continues to be so. That is provided by the companion volume to this publication, *Flying Scotsman: A Legend Reborn* by Brian Sharpe – details of how to obtain a copy are available on page 126.

This publication deals with *Flying Scotsman's*

long-awaited latest comeback in 2016, but a potted history is included in this chapter to place the proceedings in context.

With any book on the subject, a primary distinction has to be made between *Flying Scotsman* the locomotive and the 'Flying Scotsman' named train, of which No. 4472/60103 was only one of numerous locomotives and traction units that hauled it.

The express passenger train service running over the East Coast Main Line

ABOVE: An Edwardian postcard view of the train then unofficially known as the 'Flying Scotsman' passing Hadley Wood. ROBIN JONES COLLECTION

ABOVE: A Tuck's oilette view of A1 No. 4476 *Royal Lancer* heading the 'Flying Scotsman'. ROBIN JONES COLLECTION

between Edinburgh and London dates back to 1860, when the three east coast companies, the Great Northern, the North Eastern and the North British railways, established the East Coast Joint Stock pool of carriages for through services using common vehicles. Two years later, the first 'Special Scotch Express' ran, with simultaneous departures at 10am from the GNR's King's Cross terminus and the North British Railway's Edinburgh Waverley. The original journey took 10½ hours, but increasing competition from the rival West Coast route from Euston via Crewe and Carlisle to Glasgow and Edinburgh (run by the London & North Western and the Caledonian railways) and improvements in railway technology saw this time cut to 8½ hours by the time of the first Race to the North in 1888.

The Races to the North was the nickname given by the press in two summers, in 1888 and 1895, when east and west coast trains belonging to different companies would literally race each other from London to Scotland over the two main trunk routes. The 'races' were never official and publicly the companies denied that what happened was racing at all. The desire to cut the journey times between the capital cities prompted development in locomotive technology, notably the GNR's Patrick Stirling singles which appeared in 1870 and Henry's Ivatt C1 Atlantics – the first British 4-4-2 – which made their debut on the east coast in 1897.

However, public opinion against racing trains turned sharply after the Preston crash of August 15, 1896, when the 8pm express from Euston to Scotland derailed as it passed through the station in the middle of the night. Fortunately it was lightly loaded and only one of its 16 passengers was killed, a very low figure in terms of rail accidents of the day, but nonetheless it heightened mass public concern about travelling at speed, a subject which then for the best part of three decades became a taboo subject among railway companies.

From 1896, the east coast London to Scotland train was modernised, with new features including corridors between carriages, heating, and dining cars. As passengers could now take luncheon on the train, the York stop was reduced to 15 minutes, but the end-to-end journey time remained 8½ hours. The train has been unofficially known as the 'Flying Scotsman' since the 1870s, but the year after the Grouping of 1923, it was officially adopted by the newly formed London & North Eastern Railway.

BELOW: *Flying Scotsman* with its support coach heads through Abbots Ripton north of Huntingdon en route to London on February 24, 2016, the day before its official comeback run. ROBIN JONES

Gresley designs his first Pacifics

ABOVE: The first Gresley Pacific: A1 No. 1470 *Great Northern* as new. ROBIN JONES COLLECTION

In 1911, Nigel Gresley had become chief mechanical engineer of the GNR and began drawing plans for a locomotive type that would better the Ivatt large-boilered Atlantics, and he looked at the American 4-6-2s or Pacifics.

Nobody knows for sure where the name Pacific originated as far as steam locomotives are concerned. The design was a natural enlargement of the existing Baldwin 4-4-2 Atlantic type. It had become a convention that new wheel arrangements were named for, or named by, the railroad which first used the type in the US, in this instance the Missouri Pacific Railroad in 1902.

In 1915, Gresley produced plans for an elongated version of the Ivatt Atlantic design with four cylinders, but then switched his attention to what he thought was a far better arrangement, that of the Pennsylvania Railroad's K4 Pacific which had appeared the year before. Basically, he took elements of the K4 blueprint to design a modern Pacific locomotive.

Gresley did not design the first British Pacific. That honour goes to the Great Western Railway's George Jackson Churchward, who in 1908 oversaw the production of No. 111 *The Great Bear*, a unique company flagship locomotive which proved somewhat disappointing and which was limited in its route availability.

Gresley's first two GNR A1 Pacifics, Nos. 1470 *Great Northern* and 1471 *Sir Frederick Banbury* appeared in 1922, and the company board was so impressed that another 10 were ordered. They were under construction at Doncaster Works at the time of the formation of the LNER, which also appointed Gresley as its chief mechanical engineer. He adopted his A1 Pacific design as

the standard express passenger locomotive for the LNER main line, and 51 were built between 1923-25, the third of which was GNR No. 1472, (LNER 4472) *Flying Scotsman*, which emerged from Doncaster Works in February 1923, as serial number 1564.

It was named after the London to Scotland express, at the same time it became officially known as the 'Flying Scotsman' and, to publicise the train, was displayed at the British Empire Exhibition at Wembley in 1924 and again in 1925.

Following valve gear modifications, the A1 locomotive's coal consumption was drastically reduced and it was thus found possible to run the service non-stop with a heavy train on one

tender full of coal. That meant that the LNER could better the eight hours 15 minutes that had been agreed with the west coast rivals following the end of the last Race to the North. Ten A1s and their improved successors the A3s (most A1s including No. 4472 were rebuilt into A3s) were designated for use on the 'Flying Scotsman', including No. 4472. They were each given corridor tenders (each with a coal capacity of nine tons instead of eight) to circumvent footplate crew fatigue by enabling a replacement driver and fireman to take over halfway without stopping the train.

The new train had improved catering and other on-board services, including a barber's shop.

ABOVE: *Flying Scotsman* at the British Empire Exhibition at Wembley in 1924. NRM

The first two records

No. 4472 was chosen to haul the first of its namesake train's nonstop runs over the 392 miles from King's Cross to Edinburgh on May 1, 1928.

At the time it was a record time for a scheduled service, but rivals the London Midland & Scottish Railway had stolen a march four days earlier, running the 'Royal Scot' nonstop the 399 miles from Euston to Edinburgh as a one-off publicity stunt.

The following year, No. 4472 appeared in the film The Flying Scotsman. The Races to the North were back on, and the limited speed agreement was torn up in 1932, taking the

journey time for the 'Flying Scotsman' down to seven hours 30 minutes, and by 1938 to seven hours 20 minutes.

On November 30, 1934, driven by Bill Sparshatt and running a test train down the aforementioned Stoke Bank, *Flying Scotsman* became the first locomotive to be officially recorded as having reached 100mph, and earned a place in the land-speed record for railed vehicles. In doing so, No. 4472 made not only the fastest long-distance run that has ever been performed on the metals of any British railway, but probably the fastest journey of its length ever made by steam.

A four-coach train was hauled over the 185.8 miles from King's Cross to Leeds in 152 minutes, and six coaches were worked back in 157 minutes on the same day. The 250-mile round trip was covered at an average of 80mph, with 40 miles at an average of 90mph, and for a distance of 600 yards, the magical 100mph.

The key word here is 'official', because other locomotives had been said to have run at 100mph before.

In 1899, a series of high-speed test runs took place on the Lancashire & Yorkshire Railway's Liverpool Exchange-Southport line using locomotives from John Aspinall's newly introduced 'High Flyer' 4-4-2 class. It was reported that on July 15, 1899 one such train was formed of Southport-based No 1392 and five coaches. Timed to leave Liverpool Exchange at 2.51pm, it was recorded as passing milepost 17 in 12 minutes 45 seconds.

That gives a start-to-pass speed of 80mph but, given the permanent 20mph restriction at Bank Hall and the 65mph restriction at Waterloo, the suggestion has been made that this train attained 100mph.

The L&Y never published details or timings of this test run. It is only because passing times were 'unofficially' noted by local enthusiasts that the 100mph claim is known at all.

In his volume The Lancashire & Yorkshire Railway (Ian Allan, 1956), researcher Eric Mason referred to another of the 4-4-2 class, No 1417 – the test engine for George Hughes' back pressure release valves – which became the centre of urban legends over its performances, and wrote: "Whilst there is no confirmation of an alleged 117mph near Kirkby, there is no doubt whatsoever that the engine did perform some really fast running in the capable hands of driver J Chapman of Newton Heath."

However, infinitely better known is the claim that Churchward's GWR 4-4-0 No. 3440 *City of Truro* reached 102.3mph on Wellington Bank in

ABOVE: Two Pacifics, different sizes: A1 No. 4472 *Flying Scotsman* alongside Romney Hythe & Dymchurch Railway 15in gauge No. 7 *Typhoon* at King's Cross depot in 1927. ROBIN JONES COLLECTION

Somerset with the 'Ocean Mails special' from Plymouth to Paddington.

A report of the 100mph appeared in a newspaper the following day, after a mail van worker on board conducted some unofficial timings of his own, but the report went unnoticed by the rest of the world's media.

Conscious of the public concern over speeding trains in the wake of the Preston disaster, the GWR did not even acknowledge the fact until nearly four years later. Charles Rous-Martin, who recorded the speed on board the footplate, at first restricted his reporting of the speed achieved during the event to the

minimum of 62mph logged on the ascent of Whiteball summit. It was only in the edition of *The Railway Magazine* in December 1907 – nearly four years after the event – that the alleged speed of 102.3mph appeared publicly for the first time, and even then was not attributed to a particular engine.

However, transport technology had entered a different era in the age of *Flying Scotsman*, and a golden age of luxury and fast travel by train had dawned. The publicity-conscious LNER was only too happy to make as much as possible out of No. 4472's feat, and immortalised the locomotive in the process.

Life after Stoke Bank

No. 4472 ran with its corridor tender between April 1928 and October 1936. In July 1938, it was paired with a streamlined non-corridor tender, and ran with this type until withdrawal.

Gresley's A3 Pacifics, an updated version of his A1s, first appeared on August 22, 1928, and on January 4, 1947, *Flying Scotsman* was outshopped again from Doncaster Works after conversion to an A3. The major modification included a boiler with the long 'banjo' dome of the type that it carries today.

By this time it had been renumbered twice. Under Edward Thompson's comprehensive renumbering scheme for the LNER, it became No. 502 in January 1946; in May the same year, under an amendment to that plan, it become No. 103. Following nationalisation on January 1, 1948, it became No. 60103 in December that year.

Between June 5, 1950 and July 4, 1954, and between December 26, 1954 and September 1, 1957, it was allocated to Leicester Central shed, hauling trains from Nottingham Victoria to Marylebone on the Great Central Railway's London Extension.

All A3 Pacifics were subsequently fitted with a double Kylchap chimney to improve performance and economy, but the downside was soft exhaust and smoke drift that tended to obscure the driver's forward vision.

A solution was found in the form of German-type smoke deflectors which were fitted to the class from 1960, radically changing the A3s' appearance. It is in this form that *Flying Scotsman* emerged from overhaul in 2016.

However, the British Railways Modernisation Plan of 1956 had signalled the end for steam, and its replacement by diesel and electric traction. The first A3 to be withdrawn was No. 60104 *Solario* in 1959, followed by Nos. 60095 *Flamingo* and 60055 *Woolwinder* in 1961.

In 1962, with other class members still operating on express passenger work, British

Railways announced that it would scrap *Flying Scotsman*, and its last scheduled run took place on January 14, 1963.

The last class member to be withdrawn by British Railways was No. 60052, *Prince Palatine* in January 1966.

ABOVE: *Flying Scotsman* heads the 'Flying Scotsman' out of King's Cross in the Thirties. ROBIN JONES COLLECTION

ABOVE: Haulage of the 'Flying Scotsman' was by no means always the exclusive domain of the A1, A3 and A4 Pacifics. Nigel Gresley's unique W1 4-6-4 No. 10000, also known as the 'Hush-Hush' due to its secrecy and 'Galloping Sausage' because of its shape, was an experimental steam locomotive fitted with a high pressure water-tube boiler. It is seen leaving Edinburgh Waverley station with the famous named train. Not deemed a success, it was rebuilt in 1936 with a conventional boiler and three simple expansion cylinders. ROBIN JONES COLLECTION

▶

Saved from the scrapyard

A group called Save Our Scotsman hurriedly drew up plans to buy No. 4472, but in those early days of railway preservation, were unable to raise the £3000 asking price, the scrap value of the locomotive.

In stepped businessman enthusiast Alan Pegler, who had saved the Ffestiniog Railway in 1954, and who had first seen *Flying Scotsman* at the Wembley exhibition in 1924.

In 1961 he received £70,000 for his shareholding when Northern Rubber was sold to Pegler's Valves, a company started by his grandfather.

With spare cash on his hands, he bought *Flying Scotsman* outright, straight out of British Railways serviced.

Over the years that followed, he ploughed much of his money into having the locomotive restored at its Doncaster Works birthplace, as closely as possible to its LNER condition, in that company's livery.

The German-style smoke deflectors were removed, the double chimney was replaced by a single chimney, and once again No. 4472 – to which it reverted – was paired with a corridor tender.

He then persuaded the British Railways board to allow him to use *Flying Scotsman* as enthusiasts' specials, including a nonstop London to Edinburgh run in 1968, the year steam haulage officially ended on the national network. Because modernisation saw facilities for serving steam locomotives being ripped out all over the system, in 1966 he bought a second corridor tender for use as an extra water carrier. Indeed, after British Rail imposed a ban on steam, No. 4472 was the only steam locomotive permitted to run on the national network.

ABOVE: In good hands again: at King's Cross in 1963, businessman Alan Pegler stands on the front of *Flying Scotsman*, in its latter-day British Railways guise with smoke deflectors, after buying it. NRM

Stranded in the States

In 1969, No. 4472 and a set of Pullman coaches were shipped across the Atlantic to embark on a highly ambitious tour of Canada and the US to promote British goods and services.

Flying Scotsman had to take on a different guise to run across North America. To comply with local railway regulations it was fitted with a cowcatcher, bell, buckeye couplings, American-style whistle, air brakes, and high-intensity headlamp.

The tour began in Boston, Massachusetts, and ran to New York, Washington and Dallas in 1969, from Texas to Wisconsin and Montreal in 1970, and from Toronto to San Francisco in 1971, a total of 15,400 miles.

Harold Wilson's Labour Government's financial support for the tour was withdrawn by Prime Minister Edward Heath's Conservative Government in 1970. However, Pegler decided to continue running it in 1970. By the end of

BELOW: *Flying Scotsman* with its two tenders and cowcatchers ready in Darlington for the ill-fated US tour. B MILNES*

that year, the tour had gone broke, leaving the locomotive's owner £132,000 in debt and the A3 stored at an army depot to keep it out of reach of creditors. Pegler was bankrupted and returned to England only by working his passage home in 1971 from San Francisco on a P&O cruise ship as an entertainer, giving lectures about trains and how steam engines worked.

Again, concern in the UK was sounded regarding the potential fate of the A3. This time, the saviour was multi-millionaire enthusiast William McAlpine, a director of the construction company Sir Robert McAlpine, who bought it for £25,000 direct from the finance company in San Francisco docks and returned it to Britain. After having it restored at Derby Works, in 1973 he ran it on Paignton & Dartmouth Steam Railway in the summer of 1973. It was then moved to the Steamtown Museum at Carnforth, which became its base for a series of main line tours. December 1977 saw No. 4472 enter the Vickers Engineering Works in Barrow-in-Furness for heavy repairs, including the fitting of an unused replacement boiler.

ABOVE: *Flying Scotsman* hauls its Pullman train run along Fisherman's Wharf in San Francisco on March 1, 1972. DREW JACKSICH*

A new record in Australia

ABOVE: *Flying Scotsman* at Seymour station, Victoria, in 1989, equipped with electric lighting and air brakes for operation on Australian railways.

Flying Scotsman was booked to take part in Australia's bicentennial celebrations in 1988, in place of the requested *Mallard,* 50 years after its world steam record run. It became a centrepiece of the Aus Steam '88 event that October, and also ran a series of railtours including a return transcontinental run from Sydney to Perth via Alice Springs, in which it became the first steam locomotive to travel on the new Central Australia Railway. While Down Under, it was reunited in Perth with GWR 4-6-0 No. 4079 *Pendennis Castle*, which it had stood alongside at the Wembley exhibition of 1924 and which had been sold by William McAlpine to an Australian mining company.

On August 8, 1989, *Flying Scotsman* set another record en route to Alice Springs from Melbourne, when it ran from Parkes to Broken Hill nonstop, the longest such run by a steam locomotive ever recorded. On the trip it also broke its own haulage record, heading a 735-ton train over the 490 miles between Tarcoola and Alice Springs.

This time round, there was no threat of it being stranded abroad, and it returned to Britain in 1990. After its main line certificate ran out in 1993, it ran on heritage railways. It was returned to its latter-day British Railways appearance with the refitting of the smoke deflectors and double chimney, and repainted in Brunswick green livery.

The Marchington era

By 1995, *Flying Scotsman* was owned by a consortium that not only included McAlpine, by then Sir William McAlpine, but also pop mogul Pete Waterman, but was in pieces at Southall depot, with funds to restore it to main line condition in short supply. The following year, the late pharmaceuticals entrepreneur Dr Tony Marchington came to the rescue, bought it and over the next three years, spent £1 million on restoring it under the helm of engineer Roland Kennington. In LNER apple green livery and at first minus the smoke deflectors, it made its comeback run on July 4, 1999, when, according to one police spokesman, "around a million" people gathered alongside the East Coast Main Line to watch its journey from King's Cross to York.

After a period of operation on the national network, Marchington drew up plans for a Flying Scotsman Village, firstly at a site near Ambergate in Derbyshire and then in Edinburgh, and Flying Scotsman plc was floated on the junior stock exchange OFEX. But Edinburgh City Council turned down the plans, and in September 2003 Marchington was declared bankrupt. In October 2003, the company announced losses of £474,619, and

said it did not have sufficient finance to trade after April 2004, and its shares were suspended from OFEX. *Heritage Railway* magazine

subsequently discovered that *Flying Scotsman* was being quietly offered for sale – through a luxury second-hand car dealership.

ABOVE: Following its £1 million rebuild under Dr Tony Marchington, *Flying Scotsman* prepares to depart King's Cross with its comeback run on July 4, 1999. ROBIN JONES

Public ownership

ABOVE: *Flying Scotsman* at Leamington Spa in October 2005. ROBIN JONES

ABOVE: Alan Pegler interviewed by TV alongside *Flying Scotsman* at the opening of the Railfest 2004 event at the National Railway Museum. ROBIN JONES

In February 2004, a debt agency acting on behalf of Flying Scotsman plc announced a sealed-bid auction for the locomotive in early April. Concern grew that the world's most famous locomotive could be sold abroad, never to return, and the National Railway Museum successfully bid £2.31 million, the money coming from a nationwide public appeal to ordinary people, a £1.8 million grant from the National Heritage Memorial Fund, £70,000 raised by the *Yorkshire Post* newspaper and Virgin Trains founder Richard Branson matching the £350,000 in public donations.

The sale included the spare A3 boiler used by No. 4472 from 1965-78, the one on the locomotive as bought being from an A4.

Flying Scotsman arrived in York to open the museum's hugely successful Railfest 2004 event, which marked 200 years since Cornish mining engineer Richard Trevithick gave the first public demonstration of a steam locomotive. Afterwards, it re-entered service on the main line, hauling charter trips, including the 'Scarborough Spa Express', but its poor mechanical condition was reflected by several failures. Despite

a heavy intermediate repair, it had its fire dropped for the last time on December 20, 2005, after working a series of Christmas dining trips from Tyseley Locomotive works in Birmingham. After that, a full overhaul began in the National Railway Museum's workshops, one which would take longer and cost far more than anyone expected. The initial aim was to return *Flying Scotsman* to its original specification as well as renew its boiler certificate, with an estimated timespan of a year and total cost of £750,000, but both were wildly wrong.

False dawn

For the sake of authenticity, it was decided to repair the spare A3 boiler rather than the A4 one (which was subsequently sold) and it was sent to Ian Riley's workshops at Bury. Issues with the boiler restoration pushed back

the completion date, and then other major problems including misaligned frames and a cracked right-hand cylinder were discovered. A further public appeal was launched in a bid to raise £250,000 towards the repairs.

It was decided to initially outshop the locomotive in wartime black livery as NE No. 502, and a high-profile launch ceremony was held at the museum on May 27, 2011.

However, all the high expectations were soon dashed when, before it had turned a wheel, further defects were discovered, including numerous latent cracks throughout the frame assembly as well as cracks in the horn blocks. The main stretcher bar, horn ties and middle cylinder motion bracket were found to be beyond repair and new replacements were ordered.

A subsequent report said that the museum had greatly underestimated the work required due to the poor condition of the A3, partly due to a rushed inspection.

On October 29, 2013, the museum announced that Ian Riley had successfully tendered to complete the restoration, in return for being allowed to operate it for the first two years.

It was subsequently decided for historical accuracy to return the locomotive to service in the form that it was withdrawn in 1963, with double chimney, smoke deflectors and Brunswick green livery.

LEFT: The official relaunch of *Flying Scotsman* on the turntable in the Great Hall of the National Railway Museum on May 27, 2011, which turned out to be a false start. ROBIN JONES

Back at last

Still in black livery, *Flying Scotsman* emerged from Riley's Baron Street works in darkness on the evening on January 6, 2016, and coupled to Class 31 diesel No. 31466, ran to Bury (Bolton Street) station on the adjoining East Lancashire Railway. More adjustments needed to be done to the braking system, and for the next two weekends, when it hauled public trips on the heritage line as part of running-in tests, it did so double-headed. As expected, seats on the trains quickly sold out, and crowds poured into Bury and the Irwell Valley eager to glimpse

the icon back in action at last. Over the two weekends, it was said that around 20,000 turned out.

Its first main line run – still in black livery – was the Railway Touring Company's 'Winter Cumbrian Mountain Express' from Carnforth to Carlisle on February 6. However, a hot bearing and spring needed attention, and then a cracked driving wheel spring was discovered. The leading pair of driving wheels were removed and sent to Bury with the bearings to be examined and the problem rectified while

the engine was being repainted by Lancashire firm Heritage Painting into Brunswick green livery at York.

In a race against time to have the A3 ready for its planned official relaunch trip on February 25, the wheels were refitted on February 19 and a test run from York to Scarborough subsequently completed on February 23. No. 60103, as it was by then renumbered, and a support coach ran down the East Coast Main Line to London on February 24, in time for its comeback run from King's Cross to York the following day.

BELOW: *Flying Scotsman* prepares to depart from a packed Bury (Bolton Street) station on January 8, 2016. ROBIN JONES

The conqueror returns

Hauling 11 coaches, the A3 pulled out of King's Cross at 7.40am on Friday, February 25, bound for York.

A total of 297 VIPs, fundraisers, competition winners and members of the public who paid up to £450 each were on board the trip.

Among the VIP guests was Ron Kennedy, 83, who started his career as a teenage cleaner at King's Cross and who drove *Flying Scotsman* from 1956 until it was sold to Alan Pegler in 1963, Davina Pike, Pegler's personal assistant on the tour of North America in 1969-70, and former owner Sir William McAlpine and his wife Judy. "It's a wonderful locomotive, like a beautiful woman," he said. "She's in the right

LEFT: Another chapter opens: *Flying Scotsman* sets off from King's Cross on its official relaunch trip on February 25, 2016. CHRIS RATCLIFFE/VIRGIN TRAINS EAST COAST

ABOVE: A hero's welcome: crowds at York station jostle to get a picture of *Flying Scotsman*. ROBIN JONES

ABOVE: The cabside numerals being applied inside the National Railway Museum's workshops on January 17, 2016. ROBIN JONES

ABOVE: At York station where it arrived 53 minutes late due to trespassers. ROBIN JONES

place doing the right thing and very much loved by everybody, and the wonderful thing about her, she makes people smile, people love her."

On the downhill stretch past Biggleswade, Sandy and Tempsford, the A3 averaged 75.13mph over the 12 miles between Mileposts 38 and 50, and crowds were there at every station platform, overbridge and lineside vantage point, to wave and cheer the hero's return. There were reports that up to five helicopters were following the train at

various points. Two belonged to Sky News and BBC News.

Welcome to Yorkshire boss Sir Gary Verity said: "This is part of history. You've only got to look at the crowds. They're on every vantage point, every gantry, every bridge, even up on cherry pickers."

Sadly, there were more than a few spectators who were far too enthusiastic – and stood on the wrong side of the fence in some areas. At points near St Neots and north of Doncaster,

the locomotive was forced to come to a sudden stop because of trespassers, causing delays to the entire main line as well as its own train. Trespassing was to become a significant problem for *Flying Scotsman's* operators in the months to come.

At York, platforms 9 and 10 were heaving with spectators for up to two hours before the train finally arrived, 53 minutes late because of the trespass problems. Station and NRM staff handed out special *Flying Scotsman* flags and sweets.

After being literally embraced by swelling crowds on Platform 9 at York, *Flying Scotsman* was uncoupled from its train and steamed under its own power into the museum's north yard, for a final welcome home ceremony and speeches to mark the start of *Scotsman* season.

NRM director Paul Kirkman said: "We have all been looking forward to the day when *Flying Scotsman* steams home to York along the East Coast Main Line and now this historic moment has finally come to pass. This celebratory journey marks a new stage in this steam icon's long and colourful history, and is a tribute to all the people who have worked so hard to make this happen, from those that have worked on the restoration itself to the public that donated to our appeal to bring this legend back to life."

The speeches in the yard were given in front of train passengers and invited media by Paul, along with Dame Mary Doreen Archer, Lady Archer of Weston-super-Mare, chairman of the trustees of the National Science Museum Group and Sir Peter Luff, chairman of the National Heritage Memorial Fund and Heritage Lottery Fund.

Flying Scotsman was back after a decade in the doldrums. There was now no doubt about it.

ABOVE: Sir William McAlpine, who rescued *Flying Scotsman* from California, inspects his former locomotive inside the National Railway Museum's North Yard. ROBIN JONES

ABOVE: Ancient and modern side by side: *Flying Scotsman* stands alongside a Virgin Trains Intercity 225 set at King's Cross on February 25, 2016. VIRGIN TRAINS EAST COAST

More regenerations than Doctor Who!

Flying Scotsman is regarded by many as the defining icon of the steam age… but is it a historical locomotive?

You might say it is in effect a new-build locomotive, with very little of the *Flying Scotsman* that broke the 100mph world steam speed record for the first time in 1934 still with us today, and even less of the original still incorporated in the mean green machine we see today.

At every overhaul, plus the upgrading from an A1 to an A3, parts big and small were changed. What is left of the original of 1922-23 is primarily the rear two thirds of the frames (tradition holds that the frames give a locomotive its identity, part of the cab sides, some parts of the motion and possibly the driving wheel splashers. Not much.

Therefore, there is difficulty in parading *Flying Scotsman* as a historical object. More precisely, it is a historical entity.

If you go to Old Trafford, you do not expect to see the Busby Babes playing in 2016. If you buy a home computer, and have it for five years or more, it is likely that you will have replaced or upgraded components, in some cases to the point that only the original case remains. Exactly the same in the case of *Flying Scotsman*.

The NRM will readily point out that in this respect, the most original steam locomotive in its collection is British Railways Standard 9F No. 92220 *Evening Star*, which emerged from Swindon Works in 1960 and saw very little service prior to withdrawal.

In short, *Flying Scotsman* has been

regenerated more times than Doctor Who, the science fiction time traveller who discards his old body when badly injured or worn out, and transforms in a new one. The greatest value of *Flying Scotsman* the locomotive is therefore not as an artefact, but as an ultimate symbol

of the steam era, in which Britain led the world in transport technology. In our age of celebrity culture, it is as close to the likes of Posh and Becks etc. as a man-made object can get. Even people who don't like trains will turn out in droves to see it in action, such is its celebrity status.

THE MANY INCARNATIONS OF *FLYING SCOTSMAN*

YEAR	CLASS	NUMBER	LIVERY CHIMNEY	BOILER	TENDER	OTHER FEATURES
1923	LNER A1	1472	apple green single	180psi	GN coal rail	
1924	LNER A1	4472	apple green single	180psi	GN coal rail	shortened chimney, cab roof
1927	LNER A1	4472	apple green single	180psi	LNER corridor	
1934	LNER A1	4472	apple green single	180psi	LNER full size	converted from left to right-hand drive
1940	LNER A1	502	wartime black single	180psi	LNER full size	
1943	LNER A1	103	wartime black single	180psi	LNER full size	
1946	LNER A1	103	Thompson apple green single	180psi	LNER full size	
1948	BR A1	E103	apple green	180psi	LNER full size	
1949	BR A3	60103	BR blue single	220psi	LNER full size	
1951	BR A3	60103	Brunswick green single	220psi	LNER full size	
1957	BR A3	60103	Brunswick green double	220psi	LNER full size	
1961	BR A3	60103	Brunswick green double	220psi	LNER full size	smoke deflectors
1963	LNER A3	4472	apple green single	220psi	LNER corridor	smoke deflectors removed
1966	LNER A3	4472	apple green single	220psi	Two LNER corridor	red nameplates
1969	LNER A3	4472	apple green single	220psi	Two LNER corridor	red nameplates, US bell, whistle, cowcatcher
1973	LNER A3	4472	apple green single	220psi	LNER corridor	black nameplates
1994	BR A3	60103	Brunswick green double	220psi	LNER corridor	black nameplates, smoke deflectors
1999	LNER A3	4472	apple green double	A4	LNER corridor	no smoke deflectors
2000	LNER A3	4472	apple green double	A4	LNER corridor	smoke deflectors
2011	LNER A3	502/103	wartime black double	220psi	LNER corridor	no smoke deflectors
2016	LNER A3	502/103	wartime black double	220psi	LNER corridor	smoke deflectors
2016	BR A3	60103	Brunswick green double	220psi	LNER corridor	smoke deflectors

'Flying Scotsman' the train

The 'Flying Scotsman' train was, in the steam era, mainly hauled by A1s, A3s and A4s. However, during the process of replacing the Gresley Pacifics on the East Coast Main Line, from October 6, 1958, it commenced to be hauled by Class 40 diesels, and in 1962 Class 55 Deltics took over. Indeed, the Deltic-hauled 'Flying Scotsman' became a centrepiece of BR advertising. Furthermore, under the British Railways regime, the 'Flying Scotsman' ceased to be a nonstop train, calling at Newcastle, York and Peterborough.

Following privatisation, successive ECML operators including Virgin Trains East Coast, the current franchise holder, have retained the named train.

On May 23, 2011 the 'Flying Scotsman' brand relaunched for a special daily fast service comprised an electric InterCity 225 set operated by East Coast, departing Edinburgh at 5.40am and reaching London in exactly four hours, calling only at Newcastle. In October 2015, Class 91 power car 91101 and trailer No. 82205 were revinyled in a new *Flying Scotsman* livery and relaunched by Scotland's First Minister Nicola Sturgeon. ●

ABOVE: Scottish First Minister, Nicola Sturgeon with David Horne, managing director of Virgin Trains, and piper Steven Dewar unveil the Virgin Trains 'Flying Scotsman' at Edinburgh Waverley station on October 28, 2015. PROFESSIONAL IMAGES/@PROFIMAGES/ VIRGIN TRAINS

Chapter 2

The Young Prete

While the 'king of steam' *Flying Scotsman* was out of sight and out of mind, undergoing a protracted overhaul under owner the National Railway Museum, a very much 'new kid on the block' appeared from nowhere to seize its crown. A1 Peppercorn Pacific No. 60163 *Tornado* was the first steam locomotive built for the British main line in nearly half a century and, drawing mass crowds everywhere it went, instantly became to the 21st century what *Flying Scotsman* was to the 20th.

nder

Sir Nigel Gresley's Pacifics marked a global transport milestone, evoking the golden age of steam of the Thirties, and *Flying Scotsman* has long been the figurehead of the steam era thanks to its headline-grabbing exploits. Yet equally stupendous, albeit for different reasons, is a locomotive built to a design of one of his successors, Arthur H Peppercorn, an A1 Pacific (not be confused with Gresley's original A1s which became A3s).

No. 60163 *Tornado*, the 50th member of the Peppercorn A1 class when it was completed in 2008, is perhaps an even more remarkable achievement than any LNER original, for it was built without the benefit of a railway company budget, an established locomotive works with a steam locomotive production line, and under the guidance of volunteer officials. The LNER may have been able to build a new locomotive in months, but it took The A1 Steam Locomotive Trust 18 years to build *Tornado*, having to rely on innovation to provide its own facilities and many techniques along the way.

Today, it is barely thinkable that British Railways would have let *Flying Scotsman* go to the scrapyard in 1963, rendering a landmark class of locomotive of world historical importance extinct at a stroke.

Yet that is indeed what happened to so many classic locomotive types at the end of the steam age. Had they survived for another 10 years, most of them would surely have been saved by the rapidly expanding steam preservation movement, but back in the Sixties, it was not to be.

While Alan Pegler was the right man at the right hour to save the ultimate A3, there was no such luck for any of the 49 Peppercorn A1s, a later East Coast Main Line classic. Efforts to save the last of them, No. 60145 *St Mungo*, failed due to a lack of funds, and it was scrapped in September 1966. However, the class had left behind an indelible impression on its admirers, one which would not be forgotten…

Gresley's successor Edward Thompson rebuilt the pioneer LNER Pacific *Great Northern* in 1945 as what he intended to be a new Class A1, but the rebuild was not repeated. Instead, *Great Northern* became designated Class A1/1, and Thompson's successor Peppercorn developed his ideas and produced a new class of A1 Pacific, all of which were built in the first years of British Railways, 1948-49, at the Eastern Region's Doncaster and Darlington works. These locomotives were designed to cope with the heaviest post-war passenger trains in the after-war period on the ECML from King's Cross to Edinburgh and on to Aberdeen, which normally comprised up to 15 coaches and weighing up to 550 tons. Peppercorn's A1s, which like the LNER Pacifics that went before, also had a three-cylinder arrangement.

Fast forward to March 24, 1990, and a group of enthusiasts in the North East had an informal discussion about plugging one of the biggest gaps in the British heritage steam locomotive fleet, that of a Peppercorn A1. It started off very much in the traditional 'back of a beermat' style, but a public meeting was held on April 28 that year, chaired by the group's first chairman, Mike Wilson, and The A1 Steam Locomotive Trust was formally launched on November 17, with the express aim of carrying out Mission Impossible, the building of a new Pacific that would be capable of regular running on the national network. Needless to say, for the next 18 years, there were those who repeatedly sounded their catchphrase "It will never happen".

But it did.

The history of the building of *Tornado* is outlined in another companion volume, *Steam From Scratch: Building new British steam locomotives today*, by this author, available from branches of WH Smith or available in digital format from www.classicmagazines.co.uk – but here is a summary of its, by comparison, brief but nonetheless very illustrious history.

As we know, the last steam locomotive built for the main line was BR Standard 9F 2-10-0 No. 92220 *Evening Star*, which emerged from Swindon in 1960. The final standard gauge steam locomotive built for UK use, albeit industrial only, in the steam era was Hunslet Austerity 0-6-0ST No. 3890 of 1964, which now runs at the Buckinghamshire Railway Centre. The last gasp of the 'real' steam era (steam locomotives in revenue-earning as opposed to running for heritage or tourist purposes), came in 1971, when Hunslet of Leeds built a 750mm gauge 0-4-2ST for use on Java's Trangkil sugar mill estate. *Trangkil No. 4*, which has been reimported and now runs on Graham Lee's private Statfold Barn Railway near Tamworth, brought to an end Britain's proud steam locomotive building (for commercial use) history which began with Richard Trevithick's Coalbrookdale locomotive of 1802.

However, steam locomotive building never died out; miniature examples were still supplied to seaside and pleasure ground lines and all over the country, enthusiasts continued to build small-scale versions in back garden workshops.

The first new steam locomotive built for the heritage sector was the 15in gauge Ravenglass & Eskdale Railway's 2-8-2 *River Mite*, constructed by Clarkson of York in 1966 to the design of a Gresley P1, but there are those who would hold it still falls within the 'miniature' category. The first 'full size' new build was the Ffestiniog Railway's double Fairlie *Earl of Merioneth*, built at the line's Boston Lodge Works in 1979. That year, a full-size standard gauge replica of Stephenson's *Rocket* was built by Mike Satow and his Locomotion Enterprises for the following year's Rocket 150 celebrations at Rainhill in Liverpool.

Since these, a host of other new-build projects large and small have either been completed or are under way, but the flagship of that sector has to be *Tornado*, for what was achieved if only in terms of size is still light years ahead of the others.

LEFT: Peppercorn A1 Pacific No. 60163 *Tornado* passes Eskbank at the head of a ScotRail Borders Railway special on September 13, 2015. PHIL WIGHT/A1SLT

The business plan

ABOVE: The A1 Steam Locomotive Trust is publicly launched at York's Railway Institute on November 17, 1990. A1SLT

From the outset, *Tornado's* stunning success has had far more to do with a five-star business plan than wistfully dreaming about the recreation of a favourite extinct locomotive type.

The original estimate for building it was £1 million – but the final figure ended up being three times that amount.

It was raised purely because The A1 Steam Locomotive Trust drew up a groundbreaking funding scheme before a component was cut.

North East businessman David Champion, the project's driving force through much of the 1990s, worked out that if 1000 people could be persuaded to donate £1.25 a week (or £5 a month), it would take 'only' 10 years to raise that amount of money, allowing for charity Gift Aid, and so – under the now-famous phrase: "An A1 for the price of a pint!" – the concept of the regular donor or covenantor was born.

Cutting the frames

A large collection of former LNER drawings from Doncaster survived in the National Railway Museum and so began the painstaking process of sorting and cataloguing the vital information required to support manufacture, a process led by another key figure in the *Tornado* story – project engineer David Elliott.

An early decision was to embrace modern technology and digitally scan the drawings, rather than just take paper copies, a clear advantage that was never available to the likes of Gresley!

Providing a unique link with the steam locomotive building of the 20th century and that of the 21st was none other than the late widow of Peppercorn, Dorothy Mather, who was to become honorary president of the trust.

In 1994, she pressed the button on the state-of-the-art plasma-cutting machine at BSD's Leeds plant to create the main frames of the locomotive. *Tornado* then officially existed.

The name *Tornado* was chosen in honour of the RAF Tornado aircrews in the Gulf War, and was chosen by an early sponsor of the project. In January 1995, RAF officers presented a pair of nameplates to the trust during the frame-laying ceremony at Tyseley Locomotive Works.

Andrew Cook, the chairman of Sheffield-based steel manufacturer William Cook Cast Products, was sufficiently inspired by the project to take on the not inconsiderable task of casting the main driving wheels for the locomotive on extremely generous terms.

As the first components appeared, initially assembly of the 50th A1 began under Bob Meanley at Tyseley Locomotive Works.

ABOVE: The side plates for *Tornado's* frames, the component that gives a locomotive its identity, at BSD in Leeds after cutting in 1994. BRIAN BATE/A1SLT

A home of its own

Following negotiations with the local council, the A1 Trust gained a permanent home, the historic former Hopetown carriage works of the Stockton & Darlington Railway in Darlington, and partially completed frames were delivered there in 1997.

The acid test for the ultimate viability of any new-build steam project is the boiler, the biggest and by far the most expensive component. To fund the £500,000 boiler, the trust launched a bearer bond scheme, and because no UK manufacturer was able to build one of that size, the *Tornado* team turned to Germany's Meiningen locomotive works, which was founded in 1914 but which had continued to build replacement locomotive boilers right up to the modern day. In June 2007, the completed boiler for *Tornado* was lifted on to the rolling chassis at Darlington Locomotive Works.

On a cold January 9, 2008 day in Darlington, a symbolic match was lit by Dorothy Mather and, almost 18 years after the project was launched, a still incomplete *Tornado* had a fire in its grate. It was a seminal moment in the history of the heritage sector.

It moves!

The trust's latter-day chairman Mark Allatt, a marketing professional specialising in brand management, had the task of launching a brand like no other before, but just as the LNER had made the most of *Flying Scotsman*, a carefully orchestrated plan to maximise the publicity potential of such an event was executed to perfection. The story was adopted by the BBC 24-hour news channel and others eagerly followed in its wake.

ABOVE: The late Mrs Dorothy Mather, widow of designer Arthur Peppercorn, lights the first fire inside *Tornado* on January 8, 2008. ROBIN JONES

ABOVE LEFT: June 2007 saw the boiler lifted on to the rolling chassis at Darlington. DAVID ELLIOT/A1SLT

On the morning of Friday, August 1, 2008, a crowd of international journalists descended on the works as *Tornado* – in plain works grey primer with the A1 Trust's website address www.a1steam.com emblazoned on the tender sides – made its first moves along a short stretch of track, when at 11am, Darlington's mayor blew the whistle and waved the green flag, with Dorothy proudly standing on the footplate.

Shortly afterwards, *Tornado*, still in grey primer, moved south for two months of running in and official inspections on the Great Central Railway at Loughborough, and even appeared with a face during a Thomas the Tank Engine event!

Its first passenger train was run on Sunday, September, 21, when around 1000 covenantors and their guests were allocated seats in an exclusive train undertaking several round trips of the whole length of the line from Quorn & Woodhouse to Loughborough, south to Leicester North, and back to the midway starting point, as crowds took advantage of the superb sunshine and summertime temperatures on that first autumn day to line the route to see this newly born steam superstar.

ABOVE: *Tornado* steams for a press gathering at Darlington Locomotive Works on August 1, 2008. ROBIN JONES

LEFT: *Tornado* heads its first passenger train, on the Great Central Railway on September 21, 2008. ROBIN JONES

Running to design speed

ABOVE: An A1 back on the main line! *Tornado* at York station during its first test run to Scarborough on November 11, 2008. ANDY GRAVES

After its time at the Great Central, *Tornado* was taken to the National Railway Museum from where it ran a series of main line test runs, the first to Scarborough on the evening of November 4, 2008, under cover of darkness. There was no advance publicity, but the lineside 'grapevine' went electric and hundreds turned out to see this wonder of a second steam age.

During its testing period, *Tornado* was driven above its permitted maximum of 75mph, and just as in the case of *City of Truro* mentioned in the last chapter, the fact was kept quiet about for several years.

However, speaking at a public seminar on Saturday, October 26, 2013, the first day of the National Railway Museum's award-winning Mallard 75 Autumn Great Gathering of all six surviving LNER Gresley A4 Pacifics, driver Dave Court publicly admitted that he took No. 60163 to 90mph twice on its third test run, between Newcastle and York on November 18, 2008.

Dave, who drove A3 Pacific No. 4472 *Flying Scotsman* through 17 states on its US tour in 1969-70, told the audience of around 150 that *Tornado* reached 90mph before Darlington and again south of the town while approaching Croft during the run. The test train was being handled by Train Operating Company DB Schenker, with no input from the locomotive's builder and owner, The A1 Steam Locomotive Trust, on the day.

No prior dispensation had been obtained by DB Schenker, the body solely responsible for the test runs, for the A1 to run above the permitted speed.

"The design speed is 90mph and I took it up to 90mph with 14 coaches on," Dave said. "I got suspended on the last run for speeding."

In early December 2008, in the National Railway Museum's workshop, No, 60163 *Tornado* was painted in BR apple green and lined out, with BRITISH RAILWAYS in capital letters on the tender, a livery carried by the first 30 of the 49 original A1s back in 1948. The trust always stated that *Tornado* would in its first 10 years carry all four liveries worn by the Peppercorn A1s.

First main line train

ABOVE: *Tornado* waits to leave Newcastle Central with the return leg of its January 31 trip. ROBIN JONES

Saturday, January 31, 2009 marked a landmark moment in railway preservation, for it was the day when it became fashionable among the general public again to like 'trains.'

The day saw the first public main line passenger run by *Tornado*, the 'Peppercorn Pioneer', an exclusive inaugural trip for covenantors, from York to Newcastle-on-Tyne and back, mirroring the final journey made by the last original A1, failed preservation target No 60145 *St Mungo*, on December 31, 1965. The trip was greeted with a tidal wave of interest from national media, and saw, in *Flying Scotsman* fashion, every vantage point along that section of the ECML clogged with cars, photographers and ordinary spectators.

At York, space to take a serious photograph was all but impossible: the best I could manage through the safety glass of the footbridge was a fleeting glimpse of the magnificent apple green beast and its support coach backing from their National Railway Museum stable on to the Riviera Trains stock which had been brought into Platform 10 by a Class 66 diesel.

Even then, I had to vie for space with teenage girls trying to capture the moment on mobile telephones, who probably had never had the slightest inkling of interest in railway heritage before, but were drawn to *Tornado* by the publicity machine that had engendered its new-found celebrity status.

The crowd fell silent as *Tornado* sounded its whistle and the first plumes of steam soared skyward, as it prepared to begin its journey at 12.07pm, hauling 13 carriages weighing a total of 550 tons behind it.

As it pulled out of York, under the control of driver Brian Grierson, traction inspector Jim Smith and fireman Steve Hanszar, history being made at every turn of its wheels, a huge cheer rose from the delighted masses.

A brisk outward run saw the 'Peppercorn Pioneer' reaching 60mph at Overton Grange, 70mph at Tollerton and 75mph just after Thirsk. Its speed remained well over 70mph until it passed Durham.

It was said that the train with its 13 coaches beat the pre-war timing for the much lighter 'Coronation' named train by three-and-a-half minutes. The 74 minutes allowed for the 80¼ mile trip was possibly the fastest-ever steam schedule between York and Newcastle.

On its return to York, the footplate crew were feted like pop stars by both the media and members of the public on the platform.

On Saturday, February 7, 2009, the ordinary fare-paying public rode for the first time behind *Tornado*, which made a triumphant first entry into King's Cross, heading 'The Talisman' from Darlington. First run on September 17, 1956 and was regularly hauled by A1s.

ABOVE: Highways, byways, footpaths, fields and hedgerows along the East Coast Main Line were packed as *Tornado* made its January 31, 2009 debut. ROBIN JONES

ABOVE: The platforms at York station are packed with onlookers eager to see *Tornado* haul its first train on January 31, 2008. ROBIN JONES

ABOVE: Mobbed like pop stars, the footplate crew signs autographs at York after returning from Newcastle on the maiden trip on January 31, 2009. ROBIN JONES

Royal seal of approval

ABOVE: *Tornado* prepares to depart from York carrying the Prince of Wales motif. ROBIN JONES

ABOVE: Enveloped by steam: proud A1 Trust chairman Mark Allatt with Prince Charles at the official naming ceremony on February 19, 2009. ROBIN JONES

On February 19, 2009, *Tornado* was officially named and launched into traffic by the Prince of Wales and the Duchess of Cornwall on Platform 9 at York station before it performed the rare honour of hauling the Royal Train to Leeds, as again, thousands of onlookers packed the platforms. Dorothy Mather was introduced to the royal couple. Prince Charles was presented with an OO scale model of *Tornado* in a glass case before donning a boiler jacket and boarding the cab where the crew showed him the controls.

The only other steam locomotive to have been given the honour of hauling the Royal Train on the national network, as opposed to preserved railways, in the heritage era had been LMS Princess Coronation Pacific No 6233 *Duchess of Sutherland*.

On February 28, *Tornado* made its first journey into Scotland with 'The Auld Reekie Express' from York to Edinburgh, and on March 7, became the first A1 to depart from Edinburgh for 40 years with the 'North Briton' from Edinburgh to York.

Afterwards, *Tornado* became a staple feature of the main line scene with regular trips, the welcoming crowds and packed station platforms becoming a standard feature. ▶

The new Race to the North

Saturday, April 25, 2009, saw *Tornado* become the star of a 21st-century Race to the North, an event laid on especially for the BBC's Top Gear motoring show.

Dubbed A1 versus A1, it comprised a three-way race between a Jaguar XK120 car, a Vincent Black Shadow motorbike and *Tornado*, all designs of 1949, from London to Edinburgh. While *Tornado* could use the EML, it had to make water stops, while the road vehicles were restricted to the A1, as the M1 had not been built in 1949.

Tornado, with presenter Jeremy Clarkson on the footplate, arrived one minute ahead of schedule at Waverley at 3:26 pm, having taken a total of eight hours exactly. He ran the short distance to the Balmoral Hotel, only to find that his colleague James May, who had driven the Jaguar, was already there, having arrived 10 minutes earlier. Fellow presenter Richard Hammond's motorbike had broken down en route.

The escapade was broadcast on June 21, 2009, expanding *Tornado's* audience to tens of millions more people worldwide.

ABOVE: Very much the infant of the four in terms of age, *Tornado* nonetheless could claim a rightful place alongside three surviving East Coast Main Line Pacifics at Barrow Hill during the venue's LNER II gala on April 3, 2009. From left to right are A4 No. 60009 *Union of South Africa*, A2 No. 60532 *Blue Peter*, A4 No. 60007 *Sir Nigel Gresley* and *Tornado*. ROBIN JONES

BELOW: *Tornado* heads through Houndwood with the BBC1 Top Gear race special on April 25, 2009. DEE DAVISION/A1SLT

Train of mercy

No occasion for *Tornado* could have been as poignant as when it hauled a special train from Harwich to Liverpool Street station on Friday, September 4, 2009. The train, which had set off from Prague, was a three-day recreation of a mercy trip made 70 years earlier, when a British stock exchange clerk who had the foresight to predict the fate of millions of Jews in Nazi-occupied Europe arranged a train to take hundreds of children to safety.

The late Sir Nicholas Winton, then 100, and dubbed the 'British Schindler' in 2002 by then Prime Minister Tony Blair, boarded the A1's footplate after being reunited with more than 20 of the children he saved from the Holocaust by organising 'kindertransport' across several

countries as the black clouds of conflict loomed menacingly on the horizon.

The anniversary train carrying 170 passengers ran through Germany to The Netherlands pulled by 1930s steam locomotives and comprising period coaching stock. After crossing the North Sea to Harwich, the passengers completed their journey behind *Tornado*. Frail and largely confined to a wheelchair, the reluctant hero – whose feat remained a secret until his late wife Greta uncovered correspondence from those days in 1988 – stood briefly with the help of a cane and shook hands with the former evacuees as they alighted. Some of them presented him with flowers.

RIGHT: Sir Nicholas Winton, who saved 669 Jewish children from the Nazis by organising evacuee trains, looks out of the cab window of *Tornado* at Liverpool Street on September 4, 2009. TONY LORD/A1SLT

A new Shap record

Thursday, June 24, 2010, saw *Tornado* set a new record, this time on the West Coast Main Line.

By 19 seconds, it beat the previous record set in 1995 by unique BR 8P Pacific No. 71000 *Duke of Gloucester* for running over Shap summit, with the A1 Trust's 13-coach 'Border Raider'.

Tornado breasted the legendary summit at 43.5mph, averaging 61.3mph from the non-stop leg from Preston to Carlisle.

Livery changes

In December 2010 while undergoing winter maintenance at the National Railway Museum, *Tornado* was repainted into its second promised livery, British Railways lined Brunswick green with the earlier BR crest. This livery was applied to the A1 class in the 1950s and is a darker green colour than apple green, similar to the liveries carried by GWR engines.

A year later, while undergoing maintenance at the Mid Hants Railway, *Tornado's* livery was retouched, with the early crest replaced by the later crest that the A1s carried from the late 1950s until the withdrawal in 1966.

In September 2012 at the A1 Trust's annual convention at the Nene Valley Railway it was announced that from that November, *Tornado* would be repainted into the short-lived express passenger blue livery, the second livery carried by the A1s after entering service. The colour was based on Caledonian Railway blue livery. As such it was unveiled at Didcot Railway Centre on November 24, 2012.

In October 2014, *Tornado* was taken out of service for an intermediate overhaul and went back to operational, wearing its original LNER-style express passenger apple green livery once again in May 2015.

January 11, 2011, saw *Tornado* out of action when its boiler was returned to Meiningen for repairs, returning to traffic that May with a lipped chimney.

Between October 2014 and May 2015, its frames and tender were moved to Darlington, its first general overhaul completed.

Waverley debut

Tornado made its first trip, over the new Borders Railway, the rebuilt northernmost third of the 98-mile Waverley Route, on September 13, 2015, four days after it had been officially opened by the Queen. It hauled a ScotRail special from Edinburgh Waverley to Tweedbank, the lines' new terminus.

The £294 million 30½-mile line between Newcraighall, south east of Edinburgh, to Tweedbank had become the longest domestic line to open in Britain since the West Highland Extension between Fort William and Mallaig in 1901.

Here, *Tornado* followed in the footsteps of *Flying Scotsman*, which, on April 16, 1966, hauled a special organised by Alan Pegler to mark the third anniversary of his purchase of the locomotive.

Celebrities often experience an 18-month 'honeymoon' period after which the crowds tail off.

Not so *Tornado*, which still attracts a following wherever it goes.

The multiple achievements of The A1 Steam Locomotive Trust and its army of supporters since 1990 would almost certainly have astonished Sir Nigel Gresley and Arthur H Peppercorn and done them both proud. ●

BELOW: *Tornado's* BR express passenger blue livery provides a dramatic contrast with the field of yellow rapeseed as it passes Balne with The A1 Steam Locomotive Trust's 'White Rose' from King's Cross to York and return on April 12, 2014. MARK ROPES/A1SLT

Chapter 3

Magnificence

on the Moors!

The world's most famous steam locomotive running on the world's most popular heritage railway! The North Yorkshire Moors Railway, which normally has around 350,000 passengers a year, attracted by its stupendous upland scenery and services to the fishing port of Whitby, was chosen as the first heritage line to host *Flying Scotsman* since its high-profile relaunch into traffic. Tickets were sold out months in advance, and both passengers and lineside spectators alike were delighted.

It has no little irony that the newly refurbished *Flying Scotsman*, the first in the world to officially reach 100mph, pushing back the boundaries of proven technology in 1934, made its comeback to the heritage railway sector on a line that was built for horse-drawn carriages.

The engineer for the Whitby & Pickering Railway was none other than George Stephenson, who drew up plans for the line in 1831, just two years after his *Rocket* changed global transport technology forever by winning the Rainhill Trials.

While in terms of traction, the Whitby & Pickering employed retrograde technology, its construction nonetheless involved several major feats of civil engineering.

The purpose of the railway was to open up trade routes inland from the then important seaport of Whitby. Its three principal features were a 120-yard tunnel through rock at Grosmont, a rope-worked incline system at Beck Hole and the crossing of the deep Fen Bog using a bed of timber and sheep fleeces. The tunnel is believed to be one of the oldest railway tunnels in the world.

It took two and a half hours to travel from Whitby to Pickering in passenger accommodation which resembled the stagecoaches of the day.

In 1845, the line was acquired by the York & North Midland Railway which re-engineered the ▶

BELOW: Assisted by BR Standard 4MT 2-6-0 No. 76079, *Flying Scotsman* starts the 1-in-49 climb at Esk Valley on the North Yorkshire Moors Railway. CHRIS GEE

In his 1963 report, British Railways chairman Dr Richard Beeching listed the Whitby to Pickering line for closure and so the last passenger service ran on March 6, 1965 with freight continuing until July 1966. The line was used in June 1965 to house the Royal Train for the Duke of Edinburgh's visit to the RAF Fylingdales early warning station prior to the purchase of the line.

In 1967, the NYMR Preservation Society was formed, and negotiations began for a Light Railway Order to be obtained, giving powers to operate the railway.

After running various open weekends and steam galas during the early 1970s with the permission of British Rail, the society transformed itself into a charitable trust (to ensure the future of the railway) and became The North York Moors Historical Railway Trust Ltd. Purchase of the line was completed and the necessary Light Railway Order obtained.

The railway was able to reopen an initial length for running in 1973 as the North Yorkshire Moors Railway, and it is now a major award-winning tourist attraction, its popularity greatly boosted by its use as the setting for ITV Studios' much-missed Heartbeat 1960s police drama series, which ran for 18 series between 1992 and 2010.

ABOVE: The National Railway Museum's rail operations manager Noel Hartley drives *Flying Scotsman* on the NYMR. NYMR

route so it could be used by steam locomotives. A line south from Pickering was added to give a far more direct link to York and London.

The Beck Hole incline was re-equipped with a steam-powered stationary engine and iron rope, but, of course, locomotives could not use that part of the route and it remained an obstacle to through trains. In 1854 the York & North Midland became part of the North Eastern Railway which in 1865 opened a deviation route bypassing the incline. It is this route which is still in use today.

Darkness no deterrent!

Any lingering notion that *Flying Scotsman's* crowd-pulling power would start to dispel after it made its official comeback run from King's Cross to York on February 25 quickly disappeared as it made its first visit to the line.

Public clamour for seats on the six trains it hauled each day, running for seven days between March 12-20, was so great that all 8500 tickets – £38 for adults and £25 for children – which had gone on sale on October 26, 2015, had been sold out before Christmas. When seats on an extra four carriages were released around Christmas, the sheer sudden demand blocked the NYMR switchboard.

Lack of seats did not deter the crowds, either before, during or after the visit. Several of those who packed platforms along the heritage line spotted the occasional empty seat, and asked if they could buy a ticket for it. However, staff had to turn such requests down, as there was every chance that the purchaser might yet decide to arrive midway through the round trip from Pickering to Grosmont.

The crowds turned out even hours before the legendary A3 reached Grosmont, travelling under its own steam from its National Railway Museum home in York on the evening of

March 10, taking a route via Yarm, Eaglescliffe, Thornaby, Middlesbrough, Battersby and the Esk Valley branch to Grosmont.

Crowds hung from windows and scaled buildings to get the best vantage points, and the journey was delayed at Eaglescliffe because of people getting too close to the track, echoing the notorious trespassing incidents which had slowed its comeback run on the East Coast Main Line.

BELOW: Non-stop run: *Flying Scotsman* passes through Goathland, better known to TV viewers as Aidensfield in the police drama series Heartbeat, on March 17, 2016. BRIAN SHARPE

There were similar scenes at the NYMR on each day of its stay, which saw it run on all days apart from March 14 and 18. Bridges and station platforms were packed with onlookers, ranging from the seasoned lineside photographers to those of all ages who had turned out purely because of No. 60103's phenomenal celebrity status. Nobody was disappointed.

Spring had come early, and superb sunshine over what were the last few days of winter gave onlookers a superb glimpse of the green Gresley masterpiece in its latter-day BR guise, and those lucky enough to be on board were gifted with the sweeping panoramic views of the marvellous scenery that, Heartbeat aside, have made this fabulous line famous.

Before the locomotive could haul a passenger train, line clearances needed to be checked.

With restorer and custodian Ian Riley driving, NYMR infrastructure engineer Nigel Trotter rode on the A3 as it ran light engine from Grosmont to Pickering checking the clearances at the cylinders and back end of the cab at all the platforms and overbridges. All of the clearances were found to be in order.

RIGHT: *Flying Scotsman* with pipers on the NYMR. JOHN ALEXANDER/ NYMR

BELOW: To the cheers of the crowd, *Flying Scotsman* pulls into Pickering station. NYMR

Struck by a drone

The first day of *Scotsman* services on the NYMR saw national newspaper headlines made, not because of the sparkling performances of the star guest, but because a camera drone crashed on to one of the carriages being hauled by it.

Passengers on the eight-coach train around 4pm on Sunday, March 12 described seeing the drone flying alongside as it headed from Grosmont to Pickering at 25mph.

The drone collided with a tree, but its camera became dislodged and struck the roof of one of the eight carriages with a loud bang.

Not only was the incident a classic case of 21st-century technology coming to blows with that of the finest of a century before, but it retriggered the nationwide debate about the use of drones and the safety implications, not just on or around railways but everywhere.

Passenger Linda Wild of Whitby was quoted as saying: "We could see a drone on the left-hand side of the train. The next thing we knew there was an almighty crash. It sounded like it had crashed into the roof.

"It could have caused a major accident. What if it had gone through the window?"

Inspector Bob Moody of British Transport Police said: "The drone's camera became dislodged and fell on to one of the *Flying Scotsman's* carriages.

"Whilst no damage was caused to the train, we would like to point out that the use of drones, or any other small unmanned aircrafts, within 50 metres of a train is prohibited and is an offence due to the fact that they can cause an obstruction and endanger the safety of the train.

ABOVE: *Flying Scotsman* rounds the curve at Darnholm on March 6, 2016. BRIAN SHARPE

"We have identified the person responsible," he added. It was understood that the drone owner was later interviewed.

A National Railway Museum spokesman said: "There are lots of safe vantage points to view and take pictures of trains hauled by *Flying Scotsman* without the need to use drones, and we would urge people to use those, stay clear of the lines and not obstruct the train.

"We would also like to reinforce the message to ask people to stay safe and stay off the tracks when viewing *Flying Scotsman*. There are plenty of opportunities to see it this spring and summer, including two free displays at our York and Shildon museums."

In a separate incident, an elderly man fell on the packed platform at Grosmont, 10 yards from the A3 at 9.15am on Wednesday, February 17, before the first service of the day.

Witnesses said that the crowds watched in horror as the man appeared to run out of standing room and landed on the line.

An ambulance was called but thankfully, paramedics found he had not sustained any injuries.

Photographer Steve Crown from Middlesbrough, who was standing nearby, said: "There was no platform left for him – it wasn't like he was pushed. The platform was heaving with at least a couple of hundred people and the man took a step to his right."

Earlier in the week the NYMR had considered closing its platforms at Pickering on safety grounds because of the sheer volume of spectators who turned out.

NYMR head of operations Liz Parkes said: "There was no danger of him being hit by the train. We have no reason to believe that people are behaving badly."

Popping the question, not the valves!

After the last train of the day on Sunday, March 13, NYMR volunteer Chris Savory, 23, stunned his girlfriend of five years, Laura Thurlow, 22, by climbing on to the footplate of the A3 after it arrived at Pickering station and proposing to her, after what had been a well-kept secret arrangement. She accepted a diamond ring from her fellow sandwich maker, five years to the day after they started dating.

On Sunday, March 20, a vacuum brake problem with the A3 led to one of its specials being delayed, with a 'Black Five' assisting the A3 to return to Grosmont shed.

Two regular DMU services, the 1.20pm service from Grosmont to Pickering and the 2.50pm trip in the opposite direction, were cancelled to make way for the resumed steam service. Where possible, the NYMR upgraded DMU passengers to the *Flying Scotsman* service, once it had resumed.

An NRM spokesman said that the delay of around 45 minutes to the scheduled services hauled by *Flying Scotsman* was caused by a stuck ball in a vacuum drip cup and was swiftly resolved by the engineering team in charge of the A3.

The week also saw Scotsman involved in a SPAD (Signal Passed at Danger) incident at Goathland, the passing loop for the line.

BELOW: *Flying Scotsman* accelerates from Goathland on March 16, after passing through the station nonstop. BRIAN SHARPE

ABOVE: Spectators gathered on Goathland station platform to watch the arrival of *Flying Scotsman*. NYMR

The museum's senior press officer Cath Farrell said: "We are aware that *Flying Scotsman* was involved in a SPAD at Goathland station on Tuesday, March 15.

"We believe this was due to an unfortunate oversight by the driver rather than a locomotive fault. The crew and general public were not at risk at any point."

The train stopped a short distance from the signal and was said have been held up for around half an hour while the footplate crew were replaced and an investigation launched, as under standard procedures.

The biggest disappointment for linesiders came when the locomotive's return journey to York, scheduled for daytime on Monday, March 21, was switched to the hours of darkness. However, lack of daylight was the ▶

ABOVE: *Flying Scotsman* approaches the classic North Eastern Railway bridge at the line's Pickering terminus. NYMR

LEFT: Pupils from St Joseph's RC Primary School in Pickering visited the North Yorkshire Moors Railway to see *Flying Scotsman* as part of an educational day. Not only did the day give them the chance to learn about the legendary A3 but also to take part in a poetry workshop at Pickering station. The interactive poetry workshop was led by English poet Ian McMillan, with the students taking a look at railway memorabilia to encourage their own poetry creations. From Platform 2, the students saw *Flying Scotsman* arrive from Grosmont before performing their poetry in the Reussner Learning Centre, an educational space built on Platform 2 for school groups to use. NYMR

last thing that would deter spectators turning out in droves again.

Flying Scotsman passed Middlesbrough at 11.13pm and rather than retracing its outward journey through Yarm on its way to Northallerton, it headed via Dinsdale to Darlington, and arrived back in York around 1.32am.

Once back at York, the A3 was prepared to display in the museum's Great Hall as part of its *Scotsman* season. ●

Chapter 4

Starr

ng *Scotsman*

Having spent £6.8 million on buying and restoring the world's most famous steam locomotive, the National Railway Museum wasted no time in organising a showpiece exhibition with *Flying Scotsman* as its centrepiece.

ABOVE: The National Railway Museum's 'Starring *Scotsman*' season opened with four all-time classic locomotives which once hauled express trains over the East Coast Main Line around the turntable in the Great Hall. From left to right, they are GNR Stirling single No.1, GNR C2 Atlantic No. 990 *Henry Oakley*, *Flying Scotsman* and repainted Deltic D9002 *Kings Own Yorkshire Light Infantry*, which was named at a ceremony held at York station during April 1963. PAUL BICKERDYKE

A special free 'Starring *Scotsman*' season examining *Flying Scotsman's* claims to worldwide fame was opened following its return from the North Yorkshire Moors Railway to York, and ran until June 19.

NRM director Paul Kirkman said: "Our *Scotsman* season is a tribute to all the people who have worked so hard to bring a legend back to life, from those that have worked on the restoration itself to the public that donated to our appeals."

On Friday, March 25, as part of a press preview for the *Scotsman* season, No. 60103 was displayed nose to nose with the current star of the modern-day 'Flying Scotsman' service, the Virgin Trains Flying Scotsman-liveried Class 91 power car No. 91101 which was unveiled by Scottish First Minister Nicola Sturgeon in October 2015.

That event also kicked off Stunts, Speed and Style, a free, six-week display in the museum's Great Hall, which told the story of the renowned luxury 'Flying Scotsman' service between London and Edinburgh through the eras.

Visitors were able to board the cabs of four different classic East Coast Main Line locomotives, including *Flying Scotsman* itself, which was displayed with the LNER dynamometer car that recorded those landmark speed records, along with GNR Stirling Single No. 1, GNR C2 Atlantic No. 990 *Henry Oakley* and Deltic No. 55002 *Kings Own Yorkshire Light Infantry*, which hauled the train in the Sixties

ABOVE: There's no keeping them away when there's a green A3 around! The media cluster around *Flying Scotsman* at the launch of its 'own' exhibition on March 25, 2016. PAUL BICKERDYKE

ABOVE: Back behind the regulator of *Flying Scotsman* was Dave Court, who drove the A3 on part of its ill-fated tour of North America in 1969-70, and who also drove *Tornado* on its test runs. PAUL BICKERDYKE

ABOVE: The bell, headlight and cowcatcher which were obligatory for *Flying Scotsman* to carry on its North American exploits, displayed at the start of the Starring *Scotsman* exhibition. PAUL BICKERDYKE

and which is now back in its BR two-tone green livery from that period.

Within the free event, a ticketed exhibition, Service with Style, sponsored by Virgin Trains, used binaural sound and archive film on board three carriages of the types that travelled the 'Flying Scotsman' route to tell a story of speed, innovation, fame and luxury right up to the present day, ran from March 25 to May 8, with tickets priced at £8. Designers from Taste of Space used cutting-edge wireless technology and binaural sound to bring the glamour of Thirties high-speed travel, complete with hairdressing salons and cinema cars, to life.

The 'Elizabethan' buffet car from the Llangollen Railway was included in this *Flying Scotsman* exhibition train, transported by lorry to the NRM.

The carriage, which has a 22ft bar and eight seats in an alcove, was built by the LNER in 1947 as one of two for the new 'Flying Scotsman' set and in 1953 ran in the London-Edinburgh non-stop train 'The Elizabethan'. The carriage can be seen in the 1954 film Elizabethan Express.

Fitted with double glazing and pressure heating and ventilation, it is the only one of its type to survive and only one of six Thompson post-war carriages to be preserved. Two of these are at Llangollen. When built it would have been scumbled in an imitation teak finish.

The coach was rebuilt in 1959 and during the 1960s it was cascaded to secondary use and

BELOW: *Flying Scotsman* in the snow in the National Railway Museum's North Yard on March 2, 2016. NRM

ABOVE: The Elizabethan buffet car in the Great Hall at the National Railway Museum following its arrival from the Llangollen Railway to star in a special 'Flying Scotsman' train. BRIAN SHARPE

ABOVE: No. 60103 comes face-to-face with a Virgin Trains Class 91, which is liveried to haul the 'Flying Scotsman' service today. NRM

spent a period on the Cambridge Buffet Express.

The carriage came to Llangollen in 1988 and after a chequered career as a mess coach and as Santa's Grotto is now restored to the original design of 1947.

Llangollen Railway chairman Peter Lund said: "We are delighted all the hard work in restoring this unique coach has been recognised by the NRM in choosing to place it on display."

Thursday, April 28, saw National Railway Museum Lates, a free entry, over-18s night with a *Flying Scotsman*-themed evening offering a range of A3-inspired activity, with a fun focus on the 1920s, from cocktail making to whisky tasting and Charleston dancing to object handling, live music and crafts.

David Horne, managing director of Virgin Trains on its East Coast route, said: "*Flying Scotsman* has an incredible history and we're proud to be sponsoring a season celebrating its return to the tracks which starts with today's inaugural run. In the pre-war era, the 'Flying Scotsman' symbolised speed and style – service qualities which remain important to our customers today.

"This year sees us launch 42 extra trains a week on the London-Edinburgh route with a £40 million investment in new interiors for our trains, and it is great to see the *Flying Scotsman* back on the tracks. Coming soon, our fantastic new Virgin trains in 2018 which will make the four-hour Edinburgh to London journey the norm – half the time it took the 'Flying Scotsman' to do the journey nonstop before the war – and bring an even better customer experience with them."

The return of *Flying Scotsman* greatly helped boost museum visitor numbers. The York venue saw a 3.1% rise in visitors over the previous year to 750,000, despite the Boxing Day floods which hit the city.

Attendances at the NRM were also helped by the award-winning 2015 theatrical successes In Fog and Falling Snow and The Railway Children, produced in collaboration with York Theatre Royal.

Meanwhile, the Severn Valley Railway sold out of its public-allocation of 'Scotsman/Tornado' train tickets on the day they went on sale, Tuesday April 5, amid reports that its website continually crashed and telephone lines were jammed, under a relentless barrage from public and enthusiasts wanting to book tickets for the line's Pacific Power Weekend to be held that September.

In scenes reminiscent of a big-name rock band 'last night' show, the majority of the 7000 tickets released for sale were snapped up – with a small allocation kept back for Severn Valley shareholders and supporters – leaving hundreds of people disappointed.

Some went so far as to post ugly comments on social media about how the railway had 'ruined their anniversary plans', or 'spoiled

ABOVE: Special *Flying Scotsman* beers on sale in the York museum shop. ROBIN JONES

great-grandad's 90th birthday party', all of which appeared to be something of an overreaction. Nonetheless, Pacific Power was clearly going to be the event of the year, with steam stars old and new going head to head.

However, there was little that the railway could do. Its website simply could not cope and all of its telephone lines were continually busy during the day, with some customers queuing in person at the railway's Comberton Place ticket office in a desperate bid to secure tickets.

The tidal wave of demand reflected what we saw in the previous chapter experienced by the North Yorkshire Moors Railway, which turned around £500,000 during *Flying Scotsman's* phenomenally successful March visit. Of that income, £300,000 was profit and went into easing the railway's overdraft. ●

ABOVE: Visitors to the exhibition's 'Flying Scotsman' train used the latest technology to relive the luxury of East Coast Main Line travel in the Thirties. NRM

ABOVE: Explainer Chris Walker prepares to welcome visitors on to *Flying Scotsman's* cab in the Great Hall of the National Railway Museum. NRM

RIGHT: *Flying Scotsman* crosses the Forth Bridge on May 15 with Steam Dreams' Fife Circular tour as part of its four-day trip north of the border. The 8094ft cantilever bridge over the Firth of Forth nine miles west of Edinburgh was designed by the English engineers Sir John Fowler and Sir Benjamin Baker and is considered an iconic structure and a symbol of Scotland. Construction of the bridge began in 1882 and it was opened on March 4, 1890 by the Prince of Wales, the future Edward VII. UNESCO inscribed the bridge as a World Heritage Site on July 5, 2015, recognising it as "an extraordinary and impressive milestone in bridge design and construction during the period when railways came to dominate long-distance land travel". NETWORK RAIL

stars or

Built for high-speed service on the East Coast Main Line, *Flying Scotsman's* first block booking since its return to action was for Steam Dreams, an operator which specialises in tours in and from the south of England, but it still managed to run in Scotland... just about.

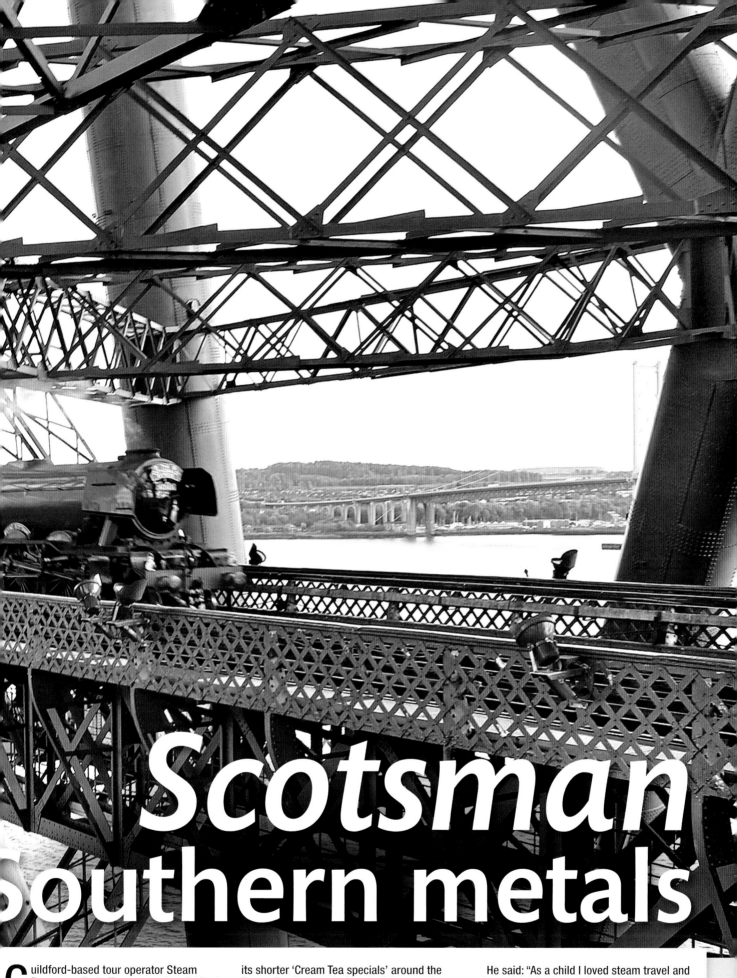

Scotsman
southern metals

Guildford-based tour operator Steam Dreams pulled off a scoop when it hired *Flying Scotsman* for 15 tours early in its comeback year. However, the majority of them ran over the south of England, well away from native LNER territory.

Not only did the A3 work several of the company's famous 'Cathedral Express' day trips from London, but also hauled several of its shorter 'Cream Tea specials' around the Sunny South as part of booked, longer trips.

Steam Dreams is one of the heritage steam era's big success stories on the main line.

The firm was the brainchild of enthusiast Marcus Robertson, whose mother Elisabeth Beresford in 1968 created the Wombles, which went on to become a huge children's TV success of the Seventies.

He said: "As a child I loved steam travel and always felt it had a magic – making travel exciting and fun. In the mid-Nineties when I started taking my children on steam trips I realised that there were many people like me looking to relive the nostalgia of steam travel.

"My wife, although enjoying the steam travel, was equally keen on finding an attractive destination and it was this that got me thinking – 'why not combine the two?' Steam travel for me, an attractive destination for her and gourmet food included." With this in mind, the concept of the 'Cathedrals Express' was launched.

On Wednesday, June 28, 2000, with more than 40 media from around the world on board, his firm's first 'Cathedrals Express', which was also the first regular steam from London since the 20th century, left Platform 2 at London Victoria heading for Canterbury behind rebuilt West Country Pacific No. 34016. *Bodmin* had been restored to the main line only two weeks previously, performed faultlessly throughout, and the train was constantly on or ahead of schedule.

Marcus said: "It was an immediate success. Everyone was so enthusiastic and really appreciated the extra touches – like the innovative menus in Premier Dining, fresh flowers on the table, the links with the cathedral and the information we produce outlining the route and places of interest to look out for along the way, together with information on what to do and see on arrival in the city."

Not one of the 13 Steam Dreams trains to Canterbury that summer was ever late arriving into Canterbury or Victoria – where someone said you could set the big Platform 2 clock by the 8pm arrival of the 'Cathedrals Express'.

The entire programme was deemed a huge success even by 'senior management' at Waterloo and the planned extra trains to Salisbury were given a provisional go-ahead subject to said 'senior management' travelling on the first one to check there were no serious issues.

The first one to Salisbury ran on Wednesday, August 30, 2000 and was timed to depart around 11am as close to the time of the old 'Atlantic Coast Express' as possible, and duly did so from Platform 16 at 10.58pm. Again *Bodmin* was in charge, as it was to be on all the services that summer.

Gradually, the 'Cathedrals Express' reached new destinations, including most of the Cathedral cities across south-east England – Winchester, Chichester, Portsmouth and also the abbey city of Bath. At the end of the second summer in 2001, on September 13, No. 35005 *Canadian Pacific* took the first steam out of Liverpool Street since the 1960s to Ely.

There still remained a major dream for Southern steam enthusiasts, which was to emulate the last express steam of the BR era and bring back the thrill of regular steam to Bournemouth and Weymouth on the historically traditional route for summertime excursions from London hauled by Bulleid Pacifics.

So it was that in 2004, Steam Dreams planned a series of trains to Weymouth during the summer season. Named the 'Sunny South Specials' they were in the end all hauled by No. 73096, as by then No. 35005 had expired following its infamous boiler tube failure at Paddock Wood, and, at the time of writing, has not turned a wheel on the main line since.

Marcus said: "Since those early days, the basic principles have remained the same whilst we continue to strive to bring new itineraries and improve our service wherever possible. For instance, we now offer two classes of dining – Pullman Style and Premier Dining – and our Premium Standard passengers are served tea and coffee at their seats. In addition to our traditional day trips, we started doing three- and four-day trips and then launched Holidays by Steam with the first Cathedrals Explorer eight-day holiday in 2010."

Scottish minister intervenes at 11th hour

However, *Flying Scotsman*'s trips for Steam Dreams did not begin with trips through the principal area of operation, the former Southern Railway/Region, but a far longer jaunt – to Scotland itself.

From May 14-17, the firm arranged a four-day land cruise to Scotland, with the A3 as the headline-grabbing motive power.

However, No. 60103's appearance on much of the trip north of the border so nearly did not happen.

At 4.40pm on May 14, after the tour from London had arrived at Edinburgh Waverley station, Marcus Robertson received a telephone call from train operator West Coast Railways to say that Network Rail had gauging issues over certain sections of the routes to Tweedbank, over the new Borders Railway, and the Fife Circle – and had accordingly issued a ban on *Flying Scotsman* running over them.

Angry and stung into action by the very-late-in-the-day decision – West Coast had supplied Network Rail with specifications for the trips 12 weeks beforehand – Marcus contacted BBC Scotland and *The Scotsman* newspaper.

He explained that the Sunday's centrepiece, the train's visit to Edinburgh before travelling the Borders Railway and the Fife Circle, had been cancelled at the 11th hour by Network Rail.

The decision, he said, would dismay thousands of enthusiasts planning to see the recently overhauled locomotive and of course his passengers who had travelled up from London for the occasion.

Those calls sparked off a storm of widespread protest, which led to Government intervention.

By 9.30pm, the story was running on local news. At 10.30pm, it was on Scottish TV.

Scotland's Transport Minister Derek Mackay then stepped in and demanded that Network Rail immediately solved the problem in time for the Sunday's excursions, and got his way.

BELOW: One of the trips that so nearly did not happen: *Flying Scotsman* passes Borthwick on the Borders Railway on May 15, 2016. The line, the rebuilt northernmost third of the legendary Waverley Route which ran from Edinburgh to Carlisle, opened to passengers on September 6, 2015, and three days later was officially opened by the Queen, who travelled with the Duke of Edinburgh and Scottish First Minister Nicola Sturgeon behind A4 *Union of South Africa* in the presence of its owner, John Cameron, on the day she surpassed the reign of her great-great-grandmother, Queen Victoria, to become the longest-reigning British monarch. BRIAN SHARPE

When challenged, Network Rail pleaded an 'administrative error' had caused the problem. However, as Marcus had pointed out, the tour had been arranged and routes agreed months in advance.

Pressed by the Transport Minister – with, it was understood, Scotland's First Minister Nicola Sturgeon keeping a watching brief – Network Rail hours later reversed its position, saying that checks had been carried out overnight to allow *Flying Scotsman* to run over its stated routes.

On the Saturday evening, Marcus agreed that he felt much happier than the previous night when he admitted losing sleep over the ban.

Network Rail chief executive Mark Carne offered "wholehearted and sincere apologies" for the earlier cancellation, which Mr Mackay had described as a 'debacle'.

Mr Carne said: "Engineers and analysts have worked hard to find a way to get the necessary safety checks and engineering assessments done.

"I am pleased to say that we have been successful and are now able to reinstate the original planned tours of *Flying Scotsman* in Scotland on Sunday. I wholeheartedly and sincerely apologise for the consternation caused by the premature announcement made yesterday.

"I will be instigating a full investigation into how this problem occurred on our railway in Scotland."

Mr Mackay said: "I hope that many people will now get to enjoy the experience of *Flying Scotsman* returning to Midlothian, the Borders and Fife.

"This however does not explain how we ended up in this farcical situation nor will it comfort the many people who have been looking forward to this day and have had to amend or cancel travel plans at the last minute.

"This is not the end of the matter. I am committed to seeing a full investigation into the reason why the initial work by Network Rail GB was not completed in time and how it was mishandled so badly."

Once back on, both trips were run successfully and with good weather. Thousands

ABOVE: The proud *Flying Scotsman* support team at Tweedbank on May 15. Left to right are Jack Prince, Clive Goult, Matt Earnshaw, Noel Hartley and Chris Williams. NOEL HARTLEY/NRM

of spectators turned out to witness *Flying Scotsman* passing along the Borders Railway heading for Tweedbank, although spectators were banned from some stations on the Fife Circle.

On the Sunday evening at Dalmeny and North Queensferry, only passengers intending to travel were allowed access to the platforms.

At the end of the tour police praised rail fans, the vast majority of whom had behaved sensibly.

The British Transport Police Commander for Scotland, Chief Superintendent John McBride, said: "The return of *Flying Scotsman* was a true spectacle and I want to thank all those people who lined the route and stations to see it as it passed."

However, British Transport Police charged eight people for allegedly trespassing on railway lines as the trains toured on Sunday. Three men, aged 28, 34 and 54, and a 33-year-old woman were caught on the line between South Gyle and

Dalmeny stations. Two men, aged 39 and 41, and two women, aged 39 and 42, were then caught on the line near Glenrothes station.

The 'on-off-on' shenanigans surrounding the Scottish tour roused spectacular coverage by the news media from local radio – including south coast BBC stations – regional and national newspapers and at least five Scottish and national TV broadcasters who, in the case of BBC1, gave the morning run a good two minutes' coverage on its prime time early evening newscast.

As a spin off, Steam Dreams received tremendous publicity nationwide, especially when cameras focused on the 'Cathedrals Express' headboard.

On the Monday morning after *Flying Scotsman* had thrilled thousands lining the railways, Marcus said: "This episode highlights the problems for Special Trains which promoters are aware of and have happened on a surprisingly regular basis. ▶

ABOVE: On the second day of its Scottish comeback visit, May 16, 2016, *Flying Scotsman* visited the Bo'ness & Kinneil Railway. It is seen in Bo'ness station yard. MARIAN CRAIG*

ABOVE: *Flying Scotsman* returns from its first trip to Tweedbank over the new Borders Railway on May 15, 2016. DAVE FIDDES*

"All credit to the Network Rail board and the Scottish team who understood how bad the situation had become.

"We owe a debt to Mark Carne and Sir Peter Hendy (Network Rail chairman) who both took time and trouble to get involved personally and to apologise to us and the passengers and Phil Verster (managing director, ScotRail Alliance) who organised some old-fashioned rail methods and skills to measure particular structures on site.

"Mr Carne also made it clear that the problems we have experienced, now on his radar, will not be swept under the carpet. He says he will investigate the current situation to ensure that the system is robust and fair by putting good systems of communications and resources into place for all charter promoters and operators.

"We are privileged to have steam on the main line and West Coast are encouraging us to 'make it simple' but in return we hope that NR becomes more flexible in its approach and delivers times and gauging within a month of receiving bids so that there is plenty of time to iron out glitches.

"One of Steam Dreams' non-executive directors, Stephen Cornish, was previously Network Rail's dedicated special trains manager and a senior railwayman who operated a tight ship, balanced to meet the requests of charter train operations in a thoughtful, experienced manner. There is no reason that his template could not be recreated in today's world to follow his approach to steam operations.

"Remember, Sir Peter Parker once said 'steam on the main line warms the market'! Steam Dreams has not lost sight of the fact that these special trains have become high profile but yet only represent a fraction of the bigger railway's business."

The Campaign for Borders Rail has called for a public inquiry into why Network Rail cancelled the *Flying Scotsman* tour before making its sudden and swift U-turn in the face of adverse media coverage.

The group, which has lobbied for decades for the entire Waverley Route to be reopened, not just the northernmost third which is now the Borders Railway, called the cancellation decision "a huge insult to Scotland" and said that Network Rail had "completely failed to understand the vast ramifications of cancelling the *Flying Scotsman* visit."

In a statement issued on the morning of May 14, when Network Rail reversed its decision, chairman Allan McLean said: "Network Rail says it never had enough time to arrange for an event a lot of people had been looking forward to for months. Network Rail is using its own incompetence to try to justify the unjustifiable."

He said there was no excuse for this failure to perform the job the infrastructure company was employed to do. "This is a massive insult to Scotland. From the distant vantage point of Network Rail HQ in Milton Keynes, this represents nothing more than yet another administrative error resulting in the cavalier cancellation of a charter train, for which several hundred people have paid premium fares to enjoy a special day out," he said.

"What they have totally failed to comprehend is the iconic nature of this particular visit, and the tens of thousands of visitors this particular occasion would bring to the Borders.

"We demand the regulator, the Office of Rail & Road, investigate their conduct, and a public enquiry needs to be convened so this autonomous juggernaut is brought to book."

As promised, Mark Carne soon afterwards released his findings into the gauging incident which almost prevented *Flying Scotsman* working the Borders Railway and Fife circle trips.

In summary, he said: "On Friday, May 13 our gauging engineers were unable to allow safe passage for *Flying Scotsman* because they had insufficient information for some of the key structures on the route(s) to enable them to be certain that the locomotive could use the Borders and Fife without incident.

"I am of course pleased that the safety of passengers was foremost in mind but I remain deeply disappointed that we got into this position at all.

"On the Saturday we were able to clear the route by taking some actual measurements on a critical part of the infrastructure, undertaking a manual exercise to compare gauging approvals given for other steam locomotives on the Borders Railway and by making some operational changes to the proposed route."

BELOW: *Flying Scotsman* passes Lamberton as it approaches the England-Scotland border with the Edinburgh-York leg of the Steam Dreams Scottish tour on May 17. JONATHAN GOURLAY

"It is now evident that a number of other key factors contributed, the most significant of these was that the time available for the gauging engineers was insufficient for them to undertake their work in a normal planned manner.

"The process for agreeing a charter tour is supposed to start with the charter operator – in this case West Coast Railways – asking Network Rail for a timetabled path at least 12 weeks before the service is due to run.

"In this case, and despite various informal discussions between the parties over previous weeks, the formal request to run the service(s) was not received until March 10 – three weeks later than requested. The request contained some material errors, which meant it was rejected by both Network Rail and ScotRail.

"It was not until early April – and with the intervention by Steam Dreams (the promoter of the tours) – that further activity took place.

"These delays were compounded by difficulties in the process of the request within Network Rail given a lack of both data and necessary resources. There was clearly insufficient prioritisation of this request and insufficient escalation internally when it became clear there was a problem.

"I make no excuses for what has happened as Network Rail is accountable for the overall process working. Even with the failures outlined above, Network Rail should have been able to recognise the importance of these tours and have taken steps much earlier.

"As a result of our findings in this case I have asked for a thorough review of the whole charter

process to be undertaken and for this to involve all the parties concerned, both within Network Rail and the charter companies.

"I have also asked for a separate review to be undertaken within Network Rail to ensure the quality of our structures gauging data is improved and maintained."

Flying Scotsman's return on the final leg of the Scottish tour, from York to King's Cross on Thursday, May 22, was stopped in its tracks by an injector problem before it set out. Instead, the train was returned to the capital behind a diesel.

A statement from the National Railway Museum said: "We share your disappointment at this news, but unfortunately some problems are always possible when operating an engine of any type and age on the rail network."

Scotsman storms the Sunny South

However, repairs were enacted in time for No. 60103 to make its planned tour of Hampshire from Paddington on the following Saturday, May 21.

The trip, its first venture into Southern territory since the completion of its overhaul, saw the A3 run from the GWR terminus to Reading, Salisbury and Southampton and back.

Steam Dreams reported that the trip went superbly, despite overcast skies and some rain. It was 12 minutes late in leaving Paddington, but had made up the time by Reading.

Again, platforms along the route were packed with spectators, despite attempts by the authorities to keep timings secret to deter trespassing.

The tour comprised two sell-out trips in one. The 4-6-2 worked an excursion from London to Salisbury but instead of going inside for servicing, headed a two-hour 'Cream Tea Special' from Salisbury to Southampton and back via Eastleigh, starting and ending at Salisbury with passengers in Premier Dining

and Pullman Style Dining treated to Champagne. The itinerary was calculated so that sufficient time was allowed for the A3 to be turned and watered before setting off back to London with the main train.

It was the first time that 'Cream Tea' had been in the title of a steam special in the modern era, said Steam Dreams' founder Marcus Robertson.

He said: "One of the ideas behind what we are doing with *Scotsman* is to give as many people as is possible a chance to sample the world's most iconic locomotive at a reasonable price.

"Our day trips are set at the same level as for other locomotives we use and with reasonably short itineraries we are able to fit in the cream tea trips within the main trains.

"Local people were able to enjoy an afternoon out with *Scotsman* with a typical English tea as the countryside rolled by their windows."

The main trip was a 'Cathedrals Express'

jaunt to Salisbury, and the second marked the debut of the abovementioned Steam Dreams cream tea tours. For this trip, the train ran before picking up the passengers for the first trip from Salisbury to Paddington.

June 5-8 saw a four-day 'Cathedrals Express' to the Cambrian coast featuring several locomotives including the A3, which hauled the train over a circuitous route from Crewe via Hereford to Paddington on the final day.

On June 15, 2016, *Flying Scotsman's* destination was Holyhead, hauling the first leg of Steam Dreams' nine-day 'Emerald Isle Explorer' trip to Ireland from Crewe, the trip having started from Euston behind an electric locomotive.

"I've never seen so many people – and children – crowding the lineside all the way from Crewe to Holyhead," said Marcus.

Altogether, *Flying Scotsman* hauled 15 trips for Steam Dreams in 2016, many of them sold out months in advance.

BELOW: *Flying Scotsman* near Hungerford with a 'Cathedrals Express' on May 28, 2016. TONY BARTLETT/STEAM DREAMS

BELOW: A waitress walks through Pullman-style dining carriage Amethyst before passengers board. STEAM DREAMS

ABOVE: Pullman-style dining abroad the 'Cathedrals Express'. STEAM DREAMS

LEFT: *Flying Scotsman* at West Coast Railway's Southall depot on May 27, 2016. STEVE NEWELL/STEAM DREAMS

Fifteen more for 2017

Steam Dreams has booked *Flying Scotsman* for another 15 trips in 2017, following the phenomenal success of its first ventures with the locomotive.

From May 13-16, the A3 will haul a four-day, three-night trip from London to Edinburgh, steam coming on at York. There will be an optional add-on steam trip over the Forth Bridge, and the return journey will be along the West Coast Main Line via Carlisle, through Cumbria to Crewe and then back to London.

On May 19, *Flying Scotsman* will head a day trip from Cardiff to Shrewsbury, and also a Severn Estuary circular tour from Newport.

Another Severn Estuary circular tour will run on May 23, this time from Bristol Temple Meads. That evening, the A3 will head a trip from Bristol to the West Somerset Railway and Minehead.

May 26 sees *Flying Scotsman* work a West Somerset tour from Minehead, which ▶

BELOW: *Flying Scotsman* alongside the Kennet & Avon Canal near Crofton on May 28, 2016. A century before *Flying Scotsman* was built, canals were still considered state-of-the-art transport technology! BOB GREEN/STEAM DREAMS

ABOVE: *Flying Scotsman* at Paddington after returning the Cambrian trip to London on June 8, 2016. MIKE SPENCER/STEAM DREAMS

is followed by an evening tour from Bishops Lydeard.

May 31 sees a slightly different approach, a brunch trip around Hampshire branch lines slotted inside the main tour from London to Salisbury.

The trip on June 3 is based on a Surrey Hills luncheon train, which is followed by an evening Hampshire Hills tour.

Finally, on June 6, there will be two tours of the Chiltern Hills, one at lunchtime and one in the evening, followed by an evening trip, again from London, retracing the train's morning route. Steam Dreams said that if the Chiltern Line is not available because of possible engineering work the trains will be run over the Surrey Hills. ●

• For more information on Steam Dreams trips or to make a booking, visit www.steamdreams.co.uk or telephone 01483 209888.

BELOW: An unlikely intruder on Southern territory, *Flying Scotsman* storms past Shere on June 1, 2016. JONATHAN CROFT/STEAM DREAMS

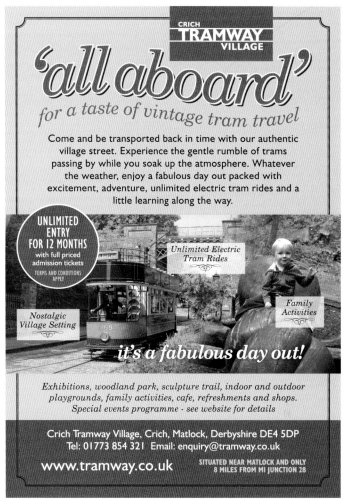

Chapter 6

Tornado: Keeping

The crowds still come to gaze in wonder at Britain's first main line steam locomotive in nearly half a century, but how many are aware of the gargantuan task faced by the owners – not only to keep it running on the national network but to raise funds to maintain it? Graham Nicholas, quality and certification director of The A1 Steam Locomotive Trust, outlines the difficulties and how they have been tackled.

the dream alive

A mid the understandable excitement and euphoria surrounding the launch into service of Peppercorn class A1 Pacific No. 60163 *Tornado* in 2009, a sage-like observation was made that has come to be unerringly true: "You'll never be short of things to do now you have an operational steam loco on your hands."

In being the standard bearer for 21st-century new-build steam, The A1 Steam Locomotive Trust has also found itself breaking new ground in terms of keeping new-build steam where it belongs – in steam and delighting old and new alike, both on the main line and at preservation centres up and down the country.

In some respects, this was anticipated within the original mission statement for the project: "To build and operate a Peppercorn Class A1 Pacific for mainline and preserved railway use". The trust therefore regards the mission statement as 50% achieved. Yet, reflecting on the shrewd observation made, the trust can only now fully appreciate the scale of the second half of the challenge. ▶

BELOW: *Tornado* passes Dawlish Warren with the 'Torbay Express' from Bristol on August 7, 2016. JOHN TITLOW

Diversity is the name of the game

Loyal supporters

Launched at the very dawn of the project, the covenantor scheme was based around the simple marketing phrase: "An A1 for the price of a pint!" That was a reflection on the average price of a pint of beer in the north-east of England in the 1990s being £1.25 and hence the £5 per month minimum commitment to become a covenantor. The simple funding offer proved attractive to supporters of all ages, allowing them to buy into the dream.

Fast forward 20 years, and the same, simple offer still resonates with supporters today (although the equivalent monthly payment is now £10 per month!).

To feel, touch and just be associated with a huge success story has immense appeal in its own right and the trust experienced a welcome surge in support around the time of *Tornado's* launch into traffic. While some of that has understandably subsided a little, nevertheless the role of the covenantor remains vital to the continued success of the project and consequently requires careful ongoing management to make such supporters feel special.

Every effort continues to be made to ensure that covenantors get the first option to book for special events and have exclusive access to the locomotive as opportunities permit. As well as regular news updates and mailshots, there is always at least one special

event each year – the annual convention, a red-letter day in the trust's calendar. Here, trustees and the convenantors get the opportunity to meet face-to-face and talk in equal measure about recent experiences and future challenges.

As the locomotive made its entry into service and started racking up the miles, the most immediate realisation was that the dynamics of the project had changed, from being a uni-directional one with a very firm end goal to a multi-faceted one with many diverse and ongoing work streams.

Central to this of course is the very business of running *Tornado* in terms of securing bookings and making the loco available at the right place and the right time. For this purpose a separate company, Tornado Steam Traction, was established, required to be self-accounting, self-governing – and more importantly self-sufficient financially. The latter, in particular, has proven to be – and continues to be – a particular challenge.

However, there was also much residual work for the trust itself. No. 60163 entered service in 2009 owing the best part of £1 million. There was therefore much mind-focusing work required to pay off the short-term loans that had seen the A1 over the finishing line, as well as building up reserves to pay off the £500,000 bearer bond which funded the boiler. Not to mention the little matter of *Tornado's* tender belonging to someone else!

Conversely there was a ready market for attracting much-needed extra revenue. With the launch publicity transcending the more usual immediate railway enthusiast world, the opportunity to create and capitalise on a marketable Tornado 'brand' was an obvious one.

The promotion and selling of a range of merchandise soon became an industry in its own right and eventually led to the establishing of a further separate company – Tornado Merchandising Ltd.

It can readily be seen therefore that the transition from locomotive building group to locomotive operating group was a significant one. Yet there was a common theme that remained to underpin the project – the A1SLT covenantor.

BELOW: *Tornado* heads through Aldermaston with the London Victoria to Bristol Temple Meads 'Belmond British Pullman' on May 11, 2016. JAMES CORBEN/A1SLT

BELOW: Blue-liveried No. 60163 and covenantors stand together on the Didcot Railway Centre turntable on November 25, 2012. IAN MCDONALD /A1SLT

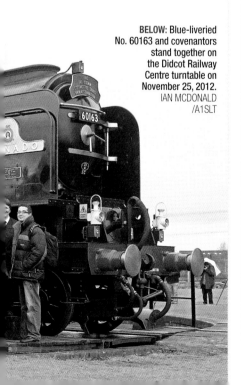

Working for a living

And what of No. 60163 in service? Working almost impeccably 'straight out of the box', *Tornado* has proved what a sound choice the Peppercorn class A1 Pacific was as the basis of a new-build. Essentially a product of the post-war LNER design team, yet actually built under BR auspices, the original type proved to be the worthy successor of the Gresley class A3 and A4 designs, being a highly capable and reliable machine, perfectly suited to the challenging post-war conditions it found itself born into.

As the 50th member of the class, *Tornado* has shown itself to be a worthy successor to the reputation of its long-lost 49 sisters. A strong commitment to quality of manufacture throughout the long years of build has resulted in a reliable, high-performing locomotive. Equipped with Timken roller bearings throughout (in exactly the same manner as five of the original build) to ensure minimum rolling resistance and married with an all-welded version of the diagram 118 boiler, a free-steaming, free-running engine has been the result.

Keeping it 'on the road' is the responsibility of the *Tornado* support crew. While it is true that this aspect of the trust's activities is little different to that of many other main line-registered steam locomotives, nevertheless it was a completely new challenge to develop a support crew largely from scratch.

In this sphere, pure enthusiasm alone is not necessarily a guaranteed recipe for success and much effort has been expended to nurture a safety conscious and well-trained team.

But it hasn't all been plain sailing. Despite the apparent advantages of being a new-build locomotive rather than a well-used one with more than a million miles 'on the clock', in reality many of the challenges of operating a main line locomotive – young or old – are little different on the modern railway.

Repair and return

After about 18 months of running, *Tornado* started to experience firebox stay failures and some distortion of the inner firebox plates. However when the winter maintenance was started at the end of December 2010, cracks were noted in the foundation ring corners.

As repair of this involved removal of the boiler from the frames, the decision was made to return the boiler to the builder as this proved to be the quickest way to effect repairs and minimise the period that the locomotive was out of use.

A more rigorous water treatment regime was introduced to better cope with the very hard water experienced in the South East where many of *Tornado's* trains were operating and which was considered a major contributor to the firebox problems.

Now part of German state railway's engineering capability, the workshops at Meiningen date from 1914 and have been continually involved in the manufacture of steam locomotives from that date. And, thanks to the idiosyncrasies of former Eastern Europe and the impact of German reunification, Meiningen finds itself involved with the overhaul/manufacture of steam locomotives and components in the present day.

In the same breath however, it is also part of the DB Engineering group, existing cheek-by-jowl with the maintainers of the German high-speed (ICE) fleet of trains. The consequence of this is that it taps into all the centralised support services such a huge organisation provides. This has proven to be vital to the ongoing task of keeping *Tornado* 'on the road'. Some significant boiler repairs have been turned round in a matter of months rather than years and, more importantly, delivered on time, allowing the trust to plan the locomotive's future activities with confidence.

A key aspect of this efficient service is the fact that the all-welded steel boiler lends itself to straightforward repairs using modern techniques and materials. Although the first round of repairs were reputation challenging, the trust's engineers have quickly learned much about the all-welded technology. Moreover, train crews of regular operator DB Cargo are much better versed over the boiler's attributes. Maintenance arrangements have been suitably revised accordingly.

When *Tornado* was due her first heavy overhaul in 2014/15, the boiler again went back to Meiningen, this time to incorporate more proactive work, and the boiler that sits on *Tornado* in 2016 contains subtle design variations from that which was first united with the locomotive in 2007. Despite this and other aspects adding up to an extensive list of work (the locomotive already having amassed 75,000 life miles), the locomotive was out of service for just six months.

A mobile home

Meanwhile, another aspect requiring attention with *Tornado* safely in traffic was the provision of a dedicated support coach, initial operations relying on loaning vehicles from other groups – never a long-term viable option. A suitable donor vehicle, Mk.1 BCK No. 21249, was located at the Great Central Railway and was soon safely housed into the newly vacated Darlington Locomotive Works.

However, this was not going to be just another support coach. Much thought was given as to what was required to best serve No. 60163's needs over and above the traditional store for tools/spares and brewing facility. The full specification eventually featured a self-contained power supply (using a small generator), fully equipped kitchen, central heating and power supplies installed throughout. The toilet compartment at the non-brake end was sacrificed to become the merchandise store (nicknamed the 'Tardis').

Meanwhile, the 'routine' overhaul of the structure of the coach was revealing some unpleasant surprises. Although the coach appeared to be in good overall reasonable condition and had been reasonably well looked after, the inevitable passage of time had led

BELOW: *Tornado* raises a head of steam as it passes through Virginia Water with a 'Belmond British Pullman' circular tour from London Victoria through Surrey on March 12, 2016. DAVID IRELAND/ A1SLT

to corrosion damage in typical areas for Mk.1 coaches, notably the ends of the vehicle. Just at the time that the full extent of the work was becoming apparent, the first of the A1's boiler stay problems came to light. As a result, work on the coach was put on the back burner.

In order to fund the combination of the additional repairs and rebuilding the coach to the new specification, a special fundraising appeal was run to fund the additional work. Once the boiler problems had been resolved and with the finances duly recovered, work recommenced in earnest on the coach towards the end of 2012.

Using a combination of volunteer labour and contractor services, the coach was completed to the intended specification and entered service with *Tornado* in June 2013. Since then it has become an integral part of the operation of the locomotive serving as a mobile storage facility and accommodation hostel for trust personnel.

ABOVE: Mk.1 BCK support coach No. 21249 on July 1, 2010, during its rebuild at Darlington Locomotive Works. A1SLT

Paying its dues

ABOVE: *Tornado's* tender being loaded on to a road vehicle trailer at Darlington Locomotive Works on June 6, 2015. DAVID ELLIOTT/A1SLT

But what of the £1 million debt that needed repaying at the time of its launch? The initial rush of railtours and preserved railway appearances, coupled with the ongoing covenantor payments, were sufficient to pay off the short-term loans; however, the £500,000 boiler bond was a more mind-focusing exercise. The terms of the bond required payment between 2012 and 2016, at a time of the trust's choosing.

Initially, it was a case of stashing away a fixed amount a month in order to build up the repayment fund; however the boiler stay problems of 2010 caused some disruption to this. Fortunately, the trust was blessed with good fortune when it heard that it was the main beneficiary of a sizeable legacy from the estate of the late Peter Haddon and this contributed to the bond being paid off well in advance of the 2016 deadline date.

The final debt to pay off concerns the locomotive's tender, sponsored in a very generous manner by one of the trust's greatest supporters – Andrew Cook, chairman of William Cook Cast Products.

However, the tender must eventually be paid for to ensure *Tornado* is entirely debt free. And so another fundraising scheme – The 163 Pacifics Club – is currently running. Based on the idea of 'buying' the identity of one of the 163 LNER express passenger Pacific locomotives (all the A4s, A3s and A1s) for £960, by the time gift aid is added, the amount raised adds up to the required £200,000.

BELOW: *Tornado* powers through Tisbury with a Steam Dreams 'Cathedrals Express' from Waterloo to Exeter St David's on September 13, 2009. IAN MCDONALD/A1SLT

Selling the name

Set against this background of seemingly never-ending expenditure is the work of Tornado Merchandise Ltd, which has become a core fundraising activity. Wherever *Tornado* goes, hauling a railtour or at a preserved railway, a TML team endeavours to be there, with a wide range of merchandise for sale.

The link between TML and the continued operation of *Tornado* is critical. In steam, on the mainline and in the public eye, the *Tornado* name is naturally promoted. Consequent sales from merchandise are ploughed back into keeping the locomotive running. Out of service, out of sight and partly dismantled, the whole virtuous circle comes to a grinding halt. And once such momentum is lost then it can be a real battle to build it up again.

There wasn't a lot about the new locomotive under construction that could be readily 'sold' in the form of merchandise. The trust always held the belief that a new-build project could not be funded by selling pencils and jigsaws.

However, once the locomotive was launched, a very distinctive name and image – a 'brand' in modern parlance – has been created which suddenly opened up the possibility of selling to a captive market. Whether on board a train, or admiring the locomotive at a preserved railway, enthused by the excitement of the day there is a positive buying atmosphere where anything from pens and postcards to DVDs, sweatshirts and *Tornado* models are available for purchase. The range is also available to buy directly via the A1 Trust website.

Away from the public face of TML lies a considerable logistics operation in terms of sourcing suppliers for the wide variety of products in the range, together with the warehousing and distribution operation to support sale stand, on-train sales and remote internet sales. Part of the solution was in the creation of a dedicated merchandise storage area on the support coach. Arranged such that it is at the non-brake van end of the coach and thus planned to be adjacent to the train, it gives

a convenient supply of sales material and the adjacent compartment offers a base for the on-board sales team to work from.

The on-board sales working method has been fine-tuned to suit the practicalities of a moving train. A sales brochure is placed on tables prior to departure, allowing customers to pre-order. During the middle of the day turn round, the merchandise can be bagged up and distributed. This cuts down the demand on the limited capacity of the sales trolley as it makes its way down the train. Chip and pin readers provide payment flexibility, with charging points available back in the support coach.

ABOVE: Seven years after it made its main line debut, *Tornado* still fills platforms with admirers, as seen at Charlbury, where it stopped with the 'Red Rose' on February 12, 2016. GARY LAKIN/ A1SLT

LEFT: *Tornado* catches a sunset glint at it passes Ashchurch on the return leg of The A1 Steam Locomotive Trust's 'Red Rose' trip from Paddington to Worcester Shrub Hill on February 12, 2016. DAVID CHANDLER/A1SLT

An entirely voluntary operation, TML provides the ideal opportunity for those supporters who do not wish to – or who are simply unable to – get involved with the more dirty and unsociable direct work on the locomotive. As ambassadors for *Tornado*, the dress code is always to be smartly turned out, conveying the professional image that the trust wishes to portray.

But this isn't TML's only avenue for fundraising. Careful control of the licensing of the Tornado brand wherever possible, plus commercial agreements with model manufacturers and book publishers, ensures that money is being quietly raised all the time in the background. Truly, the combined result of all these marketing and merchandise efforts has made – and continues to make – the vital difference with the trust's finances, allowing future plans to be developed.

ABOVE: The merchandise stall at The A1 Steam Locomotive Trust's annual convention at Darlington Locomotive Works on October 1, 2016. BOB HUGHES/A1SLT

LEFT: At Scarborough, *Tornado's* tender had to be loaded with bags of coal hand-delivered by a local coal merchant's lorry to the station – very different from the days when A1s were a regular sight on our railways! However, at least Scarborough has a turntable, installed in the Seventies especially for steam trips to the resort. ROBIN JONES

BELOW: *Tornado* prepares to leave Scarborough with the return leg of The A1 Steam Locomotive Trust's 'Scarborough Flyer' trip on June 4, 2016. THE LNER introduced the 'Scarborough Flier' titled train from King Cross to Scarborough Central and Whitby Town in July 1927. It comprised an express service from London to York, where the locomotive would be changed, before the train ran on to the coast. Cancelled at the outbreak of World War Two in September 1939, it was reintroduced as a summer-only express in June 1950 as the 'Scarborough Flyer' with a change of spelling. It was withdrawn in September 1963, at a time when the naming of express trains had become unfashionable. In 1981, British Railways introduced the twice-weekly 'Scarborough Spa Express' from York to Scarborough to celebrate the reopening of the resort's famous spa building. ROBIN JONES

Stargazing

With *Tornado* coming to the end of its eighth season of operation in 2016 and fast closing in on a landmark 100,000 miles in service, the A1 Trust continues to plan for the future.

As we will see, with the exciting prospect of P2 No. 2007 *Prince of Wales* as a future stablemate, the trust needs to think big, and several more landmarks are planned, as outlined in Chapter 15.

And to ensure the ongoing support for the future, there is the Tornado Team for younger supporters (aged 5–15) to get involved. *Tornado* cleaning sessions have become surprisingly popular. Appropriately supervised, in a safe and benign environment, what young child doesn't enjoy the chance to get thoroughly dirtied up?

So it can be seen that The A1 Steam Locomotive Trust has most certainly 'never been short of things to do' with keeping the talisman for new main line steam where she belongs – in steam and working on the UK main line and at heritage railways.

RIGHT: Young supporters in the cab of No. 60163 at Didcot. IAN MCDONALD/A1SLT

Tornado linked with RAF Marham

In 2016, The A1 Steam Locomotive Trust affiliated No. 60163 *Tornado* with RAF Marham as part of the former Lancaster bomber station's centenary celebrations. RAF Marham is the home of the RAF's Tornado GR4 two-seat, all-weather, day/night attack and reconnaissance aircraft.

On Friday August 26, the Nene Valley Railway's Wansford headquarters hosted the rededication of the 4-6-2 and its new affiliation.

Following a briefing on the building and operation of the £3 million locomotive by trust chairman Mark Allatt, representatives of Marham's military and civilian staff witnessed the unveiling of *Tornado's* new nameplate bearing the RAF Marham crest by station commander Group Captain Rich Davies ADC MA RAF and trust president David Champion.

The nameplate is now carried on the fireman's side of the locomotive.

This ceremony was followed by a blessing by station padre, the Rev Geoffrey Firth.

Addressing the gathering, Group Captain Rich Davies said: "We are delighted to affiliate RAF Marham in our centenary year with the magnificent achievement that No. 60163 *Tornado* represents. Its sheer power and presence is reflective of that of Tornado aircraft that operate from Marham and which have been the backbone of the RAF for the past 30 years."

In reply, Mark added: "It is a great privilege to be affiliated with RAF Marham as it celebrates its 100th birthday.

"The locomotive was named in honour of RAF crews who fought in the first Gulf War and in many other conflicts."

Following the ceremony those present were given the opportunity to drive the 4-6-2 under supervision and later that evening the station

ABOVE: The A1 Steam Locomotive Trust's president David Champion with RAF Marham station commander, Group Captain Rich Davies, at the affiliation ceremony at Wansford. A1SLT

ABOVE: *Tornado's* new fireman's side nameplate with the RAF Marham crest. A1SLT

Tornado – how you can help keep 21st century steam alive!

While building *Tornado*, The A1 Steam Locomotive Trust initiated a number of fundraising schemes.

Chairman Mark Allatt said: "Our covenantors are a vital part of the *Tornado* story – without their help we would not be here today!

"We are continually looking to recruit new covenantors as we still need to raise money to keep it on the main line.

"Covenants for The A1 Steam Locomotive Trust start from £5 per month, although given the cost of inflation we are encouraging increased donations of £10 per month. Covenantors will receive a photograph of *Tornado*, regular email updates and newsletters, invites to various events, privileged access to the engine and an opportunity to volunteer with the trust.

"*Tornado's* tender is leased to us by William Cook Cast Products and we need to raise £200,000 to purchase it. We launched The 163 Pacifics Club, 163 people donating £960, either as a one-off donation or donating £10 per month. We are down to our last 35 Pacifics!

"For our younger generation, there is the opportunity to join The Tornado Team. We have a club for 5-15 year olds – the aim of this club is to introduce them to steam.

"Major UK charities raise around 40% of donated income from legacies – the equivalent of £80,000 per annum for the trust. Given this statistic, legacies could fund *Tornado's* five-yearly overhauls. We currently have around 30 pledges signed, and the trustees have led by example.

"In addition to the fundraising schemes, we need to ensure our trains are full. The A1 Steam Locomotive Trust has a number of tours which are promoted and organised by ourselves and bookings are taken through UK Railtours."

*For more information, please visit www.a1steam.com, call 01325 460163 or email enquiries@a1steam.com.

hosted a dining-in night on the train's dining coaches. It is hoped that *Tornado* will play an active role in the RAF centenary celebrations in April 2018.

Tornado's nameplates were originally presented in a ceremony at Tyseley Locomotive Works (then known as Birmingham Railway Museum) in 1995 and bore the crest of the then RAF Cottesmore and its tri-national Tornado training establishment which trained British, German and Italian crews on operational familiarisation. When the Cottesmore establishment closed, the crest on the nameplate was replaced by that of nearby RAF Leeming operating Tornados.

This was the nameplate that HRH Prince Charles, Prince of Wales unveiled when *Tornado* was formally named at York station on February 19, 2009.

The Duchess of Cornwall is the Honorary Air Commodore of RAF Leeming. ●

BELOW: *Tornado* heads through Culham on September 9, 2016, from London Victoria to Bridgnorth, the northern terminus of the Severn Valley Railway, where it will remain for the Pacific Power meeting with *Flying Scotsman* on September 21-26. The tour was promoted by The A1 Steam Locomotive Trust. STEPHEN DANCE/A1SLT

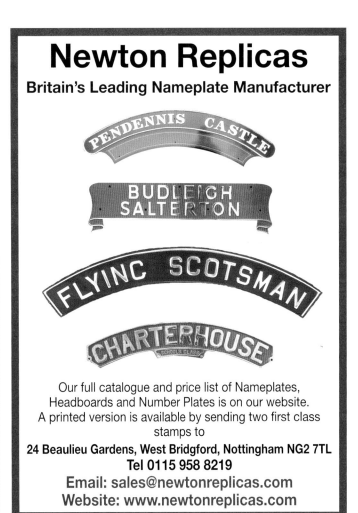

Chapter 7

Too famous

We've all heard about leaves on the line and the wrong kind of snow.
Yet in 2016 did we see the emergence of a new explanation for the
non-appearance or diversion of trains – one that states that the booked
locomotive is too famous to run?

ABOVE: *Flying Scotsman* at speed near Staveley. ROBERT FALCONER

There is no doubting the fact that for some time we have lived in an age of celebrity culture, where the words of a rock or film star so often seemingly carry more weight with the public than those of an elected politician.

The thought of mobs of howling admirers swarming round the stars of stage and screen immediately invoke, for those lucky enough to have them, memories of Beatlemania in 1964 and thereafter.

However, fame and mass adoration is by no means limited to the human race, or the animal kingdom for that matter, as the public clamour to see the long-awaited return of *Flying Scotsman* to Britain's national network showed.

On its previous comeback run, on July 4, 1999, police estimated that roughly a million people turned out to see No. 4472 run between King's Cross and York. I was there that day, and at numerous locations witnessed packed lineside vantage points, footpaths on overbridges and queues of cars parked up for several hundred yards before level crossings. At one point near Tallington in Lincolnshire, I recall seeing a man with a very young toddler on his shoulder standing next to the ballast of the electrified East Coast Main Line, and he was far from being an isolated example.

Most children are taught from an early age about the dangers of trespassing on railways, and adults are assumed to know better. Yet it

appears that safety guidelines and rulebooks are torn up and thrown to the winds when celebrity status takes prime position.

Despite repeated warnings about the dangers, a number of *Flying Scotsman* spectators continued to ignore appeals by British Transport Police not to trespass trackside when the A3 is due to pass.

Photographs taken from a helicopter on May 14 when the A3 worked between Newcastle and York were the following month released by British Transport Police to the media as part of police safety operations, in the hope that members of the public might identify the alleged trespassers. Some of them were identifi and subsequently interviewed by police.

to run?

ABOVE: One of the aerial photographs released by British Transport Police showing alleged trespass. This view was taken at Tollerton 10 miles north of York on May 14. BTP

LEFT: A photograph published by Network Rail as part of warnings against trespassing on railway lines to see *Flying Scotsman*. This view was taken on the electrified East Coast Main Line.

ABOVE: Spectators on the wrong side of the fence at High Buston in Northumberland. BTP

RIGHT: They may have been on the opposite side of the bridge railings from the running line, but these two people at Northallerton in Yorkshire were still trespassing. BTP

And still they come...

More trespass incidents occurred on Saturday, June 4 when No. 60103 headed its first trip for the Railway Touring Company, the 'Yorkshireman' from London Victoria to York, via the Midland main line, Harringworth viaduct, the Erewash Valley and Barrow Hill, when poor weather conditions prevented the police helicopter from following the train's progress.

British Transport Police C Division's Pennine & East Midland office said that at Kettering station, a crowd estimated at 1000 were blocked from Platform 2 while the 4-6-2 took water before departing 21 minutes late due to earlier cases of people venturing over the boundaries. Watering problems at Kettering caused a slight delay but this was compounded by slowing because of up to 50 trespassers at Kettering North Junction.

The locomotive was not being allowed to perform at maximum capacity and much diesel assistance is necessary to help accelerate the train from frequent stops or slowings.

On that trip, one person was seen in the four foot at Wreake Valley foot crossing, bringing Flying Scotsman to a halt for nine minutes. The individual's details were taken for a later visit

by the police. At this juncture the train was 40 minutes late.

The train was halted for seven minutes at Sileby due to a train in front running late, bringing the total lateness to 47 minutes and later, 52 minutes through Loughborough.

Now out of its path and running behind service trains, Flying Scotsman was noted 60 minutes down passing Chesterfield, arriving 81 minutes late at York.

Following these incidents and to ensure the safety of those wanting to see the engine on future movements around the country, extensive planning discussions were held with the railway industry, resulting in a significant policing operation effected and a communications campaign undertaken to educate and warn the public about the risks involved.

British Transport Police also issued a second set of photographs as part of their bid to identify and speak to trespassers.

In one of the pictures, all taken in the Wellingborough area on June 4, three people are clearly seen on the side of the ballast, one with a camera tripod in position.

Earlier, Network Rail said that it did not want Flying Scotsman to operate that trip out of King's Cross because of trespass fears so the train started at Victoria at 6.30am and took a circuitous route via Acton and Dudding Hill and on to the Midland Main Line to reach St. Albans and also calling at Luton, Bedford, Kettering and Melton Mowbray before going on to York.

Network Rail and the National Railway Museum also declined to issue timings of Flying Scotsman to the public, in a bid to cut down the risk of trespass.

British Transport Police Chief Inspector David Oram said: "In order to keep the public safe we will enforce the law where appropriate, which is why we are releasing the images of people trespassing today in a bid to trace those responsible. If you recognise yourself or any of the people pictured in the images please contact us.

"We will continue to identify and take action against trespassers on future journeys to ensure that these pass safely and free from disruption.

"Our priority is the safety of the public, passengers and rail staff.

BELOW: LNER A3 Pacific No. 60103 Flying Scotsman passes Bargrave on the MR Chesterfield-Rotherham line on June 4. The girder bridge carried the GCR main line from Marylebone to Sheffield Victoria on which Flying Scotsman worked regularly during the 1950s. ALAN WEAVER

ABOVE: A passenger on board the Railway Touring Company's 'Yorkshireman' took this picture of lineside trespassers in the Wellingborough area on June 4, 2016. BTP

"We understand that steam specials generate lots of interest and the movements of *Flying Scotsman* have and are attracting unprecedented levels of interest from all sections of the public.

"But despite our advice and numerous warnings people have put themselves at risk by standing too close to railway lines, giving little thought to the potential dangers and any offences they might be committing. Not only is this extremely dangerous, but it has resulted in public service trains being delayed.

"We have released the photographs hoping that they – the trespassers – will be recognised

ABOVE: Against a background of the recently closed Ferrybridge Power Station in West Yorkshire, No. 60103 passes Brotherton with the 'Yorkshireman' on June 4. BRIAN SHARPE

and details passed to us. We will enforce the law where appropriate."

Trespassing on railways can incur a £1000 fine.

Rob McIntosh, route managing director for Network Rail, said: "While I must thank the vast majority of people who have been out to see *Flying Scotsman* for staying safe, it is deeply worrying to see people standing trackside. Even one person trespassing is one too many."

Trips rerouted to avoid trespassers

Fears of a repeat of the infamous lineside trespass incidents which brought No. 60103 to a halt on its February 25 relaunch trip played a part in a decision to scrap its next planned run out of King's Cross.

The locomotive was scheduled for the Railway Touring Company's 'White Rose' trip on June 18, and still did so as planned, but instead was coupled on at Newark-on-Trent after the train was hauled from King's Cross by a West Coast Railways diesel, departing at 7.05pm and picking up at Welwyn Garden City, Huntingdon and Peterborough. From there, the train took the Great Northern & Great Eastern Joint Line to Spalding and ran through Grantham to Newark where *Flying Scotsman* was waiting.

From Newark, the A3 headed the train on a more circuitous route than had been originally planned, via Lincoln, Pyewipe Junction and Gainsborough with a water stop at Finningley.

The 'White Rose' then rejoined the ECML and travelled to York via Doncaster. On the return trip, No. 60103 headed the train along the ECML to West Hampstead, where King's Cross passengers disembarked. In that instance, it was not possible to take the train back into King's Cross because of engineering work there.

Train operator West Coast took the decision not to run out of King's Cross partially because of the fears of a repeat performance of the lineside trespass incident, fuelled largely by the locomotive's celebrity status, and a decision to err on the side of caution, compounded by the difficulty of a positioning move from the previous trip. The extra mileage for passengers through Lincoln was a compromise solution.

The 'White Rose' was not the only *Flying Scotsman* trip to fall foul of similar fears that the lineside crowds might invade the trackside and create safety hazards.

A sold-out Steam Dreams 'Cathedrals Express' afternoon trip booked to call at Cambridge and Ely en route to Norwich on Wednesday, May 25, was changed to run on another route in the south of England instead, as a two-part Surrey Hills excursion.

Planners said that there are too many stretches of track between Ely and Norwich that could allow spectators to get too close to the train.

Steam Dreams' chairman Marcus Robertson said he was "devastated for enthusiasts but was adamant that it was the right thing to do".

He said: "Although Network Rail has not said that we can't run the trip between Ely and Norwich we decided to do the sensible thing because the threat to life and limb is too much."

He added that once the initial excitement of *Flying Scotsman*'s return to the main line has calmed down, he plans to bring the engine back to Norfolk.

"Everyone involved with these trips does it because it's fun and for the love of it but we have also got to preserve our British heritage and protect the reputation of our steam locomotives," he said.

Passengers who had booked seats on the Ely trip were offered refunds or first refusal on later trains.

Network Rail said that it was not taking action by stepping in or suggesting that the use of *Flying Scotsman* be curtailed to avoid the risk of crowds gathering on linesides.

A spokesman said the judgment and responsibility for the use of the 4-6-2 is the prerogative of railtour promoters and their train operating company to plan the length of their locomotives' routes.

However, by midsummer 2016, *Flying Scotsman* had entered its most intensive period of main line use since its return to steam.

ABOVE: *Flying Scotsman* passes Collingham on the Newark to Lincoln line with the Railway Touring Company's 'White Rose' on June 18, 2016. Only a moderate number of spectators were out, maybe because of the late change to the tour's route. ALAN WEAVER

ABOVE: LNER A3 PACIFIC No. 60103 *Flying Scotsman* heads out of Peterborough with the return leg of the Railway Touring Company's 'White Rose' from York to King's Cross at 7.20pm on June 18, 2016. The following day would have been its designer Sir Nigel Gresley's 140th birthday. ROBIN JONES

Cat snatched from track before *Scotsman* passes!

A man jumped on to a railway line to rescue an injured cat – 40 minutes before *Flying Scotsman* passed through.

Brian Ridgeway, 68, had visited Reddish South Station to catch a glimpse of the A3 on June 7, when he noticed the distressed black moggy curled up on the tracks.

Knowing that the line was hardly used and the special would not pass through for at least another 40 minutes, he jumped down and moved the cat to safety.

He and *Manchester Evening News* photographer Andy Lambert, who was also there for the train, contacted the cat's owner from details on his collar. The owner was quickly reunited with the cat.

The story featured in national newspapers. Speaking to the *MEN*, Brian said: "I could see the cat was badly injured. I just wanted to get it off the track. I didn't like to see it like that. I wouldn't like it if it was my cat."

ABOVE: *Flying Scotsman* crosses the River Trent over the King George V bridge at Keadby on the approach to Althorpe station at the head of the Railway Touring Company's 'The Tynesider' on June 11. The Grade II listed bridge, a Scherzer rolling lift bridge, was first opened on May 21, 1916, but the lifting section has not been used since 1956. Built by the iconic bridge building firm of Sir William Arrol & Co of Glasgow, the bridge is somewhat overlooked in comparison to other bridges built by the company, such as the Tay and Forth railway bridges, having had no formal opening ceremony because of the First World War, and little recognition this year, other than by local schoolchildren, of its centenary. GRAHAM NUTTALL

LEFT: Trespassers will be gored: *Flying Scotsman* with the Carnforth to Carlisle leg of the Railway Touring Company's 'The Hadrian' tour from Leicester to Carlisle and York crossing Birkbeck Viaduct on the climb to Shap on July 2, 2016. Witnesses saw a police helicopter flying north along the line, maybe trespasser spotting? ANDREW*

BELOW: *Flying Scotsman* passes under London Underground's Piccadilly and District lines on the approach to Acton South on the West London line with the Railway Touring Company's 'Yorkshireman' on June 25, 2016. JOHN TITLOW

Chapter 8

The Shildon Shed Bash

Tickets for trains hauled by the newly overhauled *Flying Scotsman* had been at a premium, but 44,000 people were able to see it free of charge at the Locomotion museum in Shildon's nine-day free festival and ride behind it for just £5.

The legendary 'shed bash' of the Fifties and Sixties provided the basis for a grand finale to the National Railway Museum's *Scotsman* season.

Back then, enthusiasts would tour a region in the hope of visiting as many engine sheds and depots as possible to see as many locomotives as they could in a short space of time.

The North East was a choice destination, with County Durham alone having 15 sheds, including Darlington 51A, Gateshead 52A, Sunderland South Dock 54A and Tyne Dock 54B.

The NRM decided to rekindle the spirit of those days with a nine-day free festival at its Locomotion outreach station museum at Shildon.

The venue is situated near Timothy Hackworth's Soho Works on the world's first steam-hauled public railway, the Stockton & Darlington, which opened on September 27, 1825. The town became a major centre for British railway engineering because of the presence of Shildon wagon works, which closed in 1984.

The museum was opened on October 22, 2004 by Prime Minister Tony Blair. Built at a cost of £11.3 million, it is based on the former Timothy Hackworth museum.

The museum is operated in partnership with Durham County Council and was expected to bring 60,000 visitors a year to the small town. However, during its first six months, it attracted 94,000 visitors.

The East Coast Main Line-themed Shildon Shed Bash with *Flying Scotsman* as its star attraction was held over July 23-31, 2016.

However, well before the green giant had arrived, Shildon was subjected to sizeable regeneration work in readiness, including refurbishment of the town square and the installation of canopies over the old water feature and statue being removed to open up the space. Under the county council facelift, seating and bins were replaced across the town centre, with improved lighting also installed.

The improvements come after consultations with residents, schools and businesses highlighted the need to make the square more usable as a public space for events.

Cllr Neil Foster, Cabinet member for economic regeneration and culture, said: "The visit of the *Flying Scotsman* promises to be a major event for Shildon and we look forward to welcoming it with an improved public space."

The event was a dazzling success, attracting more than 44,000 visitors.

At this modern-day shed bash, A3 Pacific No. 60103 *Flying Scotsman* was joined by an impressive supporting cast comprising John Cameron's A4 Pacific No. 60009 *Union of South Africa*, the North Eastern Locomotive Preservation Group-owned Q6 0-8-0 No. 63395, Peckett 0-4-0ST No. 2012 of 1941 *Teddy* and J72 0-6-0T No. 69023 *Joem* joining Gresley V2 2-6-2 No. 4771 *Green Arrow* and J21 0-6-0 No. 65033.

Representing the generation of East Coast motive power that replaced the likes of *Flying Scotsman* and Gresley Pacifics was the NRM's Class 55 Deltic D9002 *Kings Own Yorkshire Light Infantry* newly restored in BR two-tone green livery.

In 2016, the North Eastern Locomotive Preservation Group celebrated its 50th anniversary in 2016 so it was fitting to be represented at the showpiece event.

NELPG was formed in 1966 with the intention of preserving some of the steam locomotives still working in the North East of England. In less than 18 months this growing band of volunteers had raised sufficient funds to purchase two heavy freight locomotives, J27 0-6-0 No. 65894 and Q6 0-8-0 No. 63395. Both were subsequently overhauled and transferred to the nascent North Yorkshire Moors Railway in the early Seventies.

Rather than keep its locomotives 'stuffed and mounted', NELPG's primary objective is to have as many of its locomotives in steam as possible.

BELOW: The East Coast stars line up outside the Locomotion museum for the Shildon Shed Bash: left to right are Class 55 D9002 *Kings Own Yorkshire Light Infantry*, A4 No. 60009 *Union of South Africa*, *Flying Scotsman*, Q6 No. 63395 and V2 No. 4771 *Green Arrow*. ANTHONY COULLS

An A3 and A4 reunited!

ABOVE: *Flying Scotsman* and *Union of South Africa* delight the crowds at Locomotion. The A4 is carrying a 'Flying Scotsman' headboard. RICHARD PEARSON

The event was also the first opportunity to see a BR-liveried A3 and A4 together since *Flying Scotsman's* return to steam.

The motive power line-up was especially appropriate given Shildon's proximity to the East Coast Main Line and also with the Stainmore line and Consett nearby, No. 65033 having a strong attachment to Stainmore and No. 63395 to the freight workings of the North East with a number of the class allocated to West Hartlepool (51C). J72s were also station pilots at Newcastle and No. 69023 carries the ornate livery once carried by classmate No. 68723.

On the second weekend *Flying Scotsman* and *Union of South Africa* uniquely double headed on the demonstration line. The ▶

ABOVE: *Flying Scotsman* double heads with A4 *Union of South Africa* on July 30. ANTHONY COULLS

ABOVE: Little and large: *Flying Scotsman* comes face to face with the smallest star of the show, Peckett 0-4-0ST *Teddy*. RICHARD PEARSON

ABOVE: Two of the less illustrious heavy freight engines which were once a daily sight in the North East take centre stage: J21 0-6-0 No. 65033, which is awaiting funds to restore it to running condition, and NELPG's Q6 0-8-0 No. 63395. RICHARD PEARSON

mornings and evenings featured pay-to-attend photographers' sessions which included the dream Gresley line-up of a V2, A3 and A4 as well as the North Eastern trio of the Q6, J21 and J72.

Visitors were able to ride behind *Flying Scotsman* for £5, 'cab' many of the guest locomotives and attend specialist talks. The £5 tickets were not made available for pre-booking, in order to ensure that all fans had an equal opportunity of experiencing travel behind the steam legend.

NRM director Paul Kirkman said: "As so many heritage railways sold all their available *Flying Scotsman* rides within days and many railway tours starring *Scotsman* are fully booked, we wanted to offer a truly open chance for fans of this iconic locomotive to ride behind this steam legend at our Shildon museum."

Locomotion museum manager Gary Campbell said: "We're delighted so many people from County Durham and beyond were able to enjoy seeing *Flying Scotsman* and a host of other famous locomotives at the museum for what was a true celebration of steam heritage." ●

BELOW: The line-up of East Coast motive power as viewed from the side. RICHARD PEARSON

ABOVE: *Union of South Africa*, representing the pinnacle of Gresley locomotive development in the golden age of steam in the Thirties, compares its profile with that of the most famous product of the Twenties. RICHARD PEARSON

RIGHT: *Flying Scotsman* reflected in a puddle of rainwater at Locomotion. RICHARD PEARSON

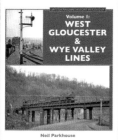

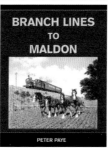
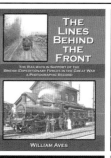

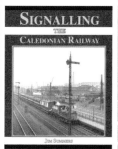

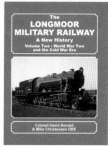
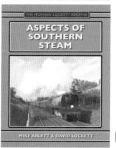
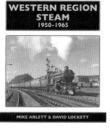
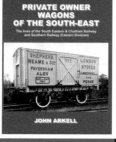

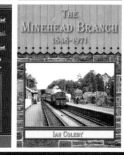

Chapter 9

Scotsman stars at Swindon MkII!

Flying Scotsman fever struck Birmingham for three days in September 2016, the LNER giant drawing more than 6000 visitors to Tyseley Locomotive Works in the heart of rival GWR territory.

Flying Scotsman's next port of call was Birmingham, a city well away from LNER territory. Its crowd-pulling September 16-18 appearance at Tyseley Locomotive Works was one of the bill-topping events in the second Birmingham Heritage Week, an event to showcase the second city's social, cultural and industrial heritage.

The festival comprised more than 170 individual events held at heritage sites, museums, libraries and other venues across the city between September 8-18.

One of the key objectives of the week is to encourage local communities and visitors alike to explore the city's historical venues and take part in a series of engaging activities which will highlight the rich and diverse history of Birmingham, known in Victorian times as the 'workshop of the world'.

The Birmingham Heritage Week programme included guided walks, performances, talks, trails, exhibitions, exclusive access to notable buildings and workshops for children. It coincided with the UK's largest heritage festival, Heritage Open Days, which ran from September 8-11.

The event had a railway launch, not by *Flying Scotsman*, but one of its very junior second cousins several times removed.

Tyseley Locomotive Works-based standard gauge Peckett 0-4-0ST No. 1 (works number 2004 of 1941) was taken by haulier Moveright International to Curzon Street station especially for the launch of Heritage Week 2016 by Lord Mayor Carl Rice.

Built by Bristol-based Peckett & Sons at Atlas Works, it spent most of its revenue-earning keep at the General Electric Co. (GEC) factory in Witton as No.6. It is owned by Birmingham City Museum and kept in Tyseley's care.

For the event at Curzon Street station on September 7, it was in light steam – and therefore became the first official steam train to return to the landmark Victorian station in 50 years.

The following year, the station also became the terminus of the Grand Junction Railway, and is therefore of international heritage significance as it connected two of the first three inter-city railways, the first being the Liverpool & Manchester.

The surviving Grade I listed entrance building designed by Philip Hardwick is the world's oldest surviving piece of monumental railway architecture and as such a real treasure among Birmingham's historic buildings.

Costing £28,000 to build, the architecture is Roman inspired, following Hardwick's trip to Italy in 1818–19. It has tall pillars running up the front of the building, made out of a series of huge blocks of stone. The design mirrored the Euston Arch at the London end of the London & Birmingham Railway.

When the London & Birmingham Railway and Grand Junction railway were amalgamated into the LNWR in 1846 and what became the more convenient New Street station opened in 1854, Curzon Street was quickly downgraded, eventually becoming a freight terminal which closed in 1966.

Thankfully, Curzon Street's magnificent entrance building did not meet the same fate as the Euston Arch, which was demolished in the early Sixties despite a massive campaign by conservationists to save it. However, for so long a Cinderella building in a back street away from the city centre, it is earmarked for a trip to the ball big time.

Curzon Street is proposed to be the Birmingham terminus of the new and controversial High Speed 2 rail link from London with possible tram links between the future Curzon Street and New Street stations.

ABOVE: Peckett 0-4-0ST No. 1 becomes the first engine in steam at Curzon Street station in half a century. MOVERIGHT INTERNATIONAL

ABOVE: No. 1 on a Moveright International trailer outside the entrance to Curzon Street station, with Vintage Trains chairman Michael Whitehouse and the City of Birmingham's Lord Mayor and Lady Mayoress on September 7.

RIGHT: Displaying the headboard bearing the name of its owner, *Flying Scotsman* stands on the Tyseley turntable on September 16. Behind it is LMS Jubilee 4-6-0 No. 5593 *Kolhapur*, which was acquired early on by what became Birmingham Railway Museum. ROBIN JONES

The origin of Tyseley shed

ABOVE: Pioneering officials of the Talyllyn Railway Preservation Society together in May 1951: left to right, David Curwen (chief mechanical engineer), Bill Trinder (chairman), Pat Whitehouse (secretary), Tom Rolt (railway general manager) and Pat Garland (treasurer). The two Pats later bought main line locomotives together and helped establish the Dart Valley Railway in Devon, while Pat Whitehouse was responsible for the creation of Tyseley Locomotive Works, which proudly hosted *Flying Scotsman* in September 2016. TALYLLYN ARCHIVES

ABOVE: Visitors walk over the tracks at a Tyseley steam open day in the autumn of 1970. ROBIN JONES

Tyseley as the home of a sizeable engine shed dates back to the last period of main line railway building in the steam era.

Only too aware of the criticism that its name stood for 'The Great Way Round', the Swindon empire set about ironing out kinks in its routes to shorten train times between Paddington and its two major hubs of Taunton and Birmingham.

The North Warwickshire Railway was designed to create a more direct route between south Birmingham and Stratford-upon-Avon, which would bypass the existing route via Lapworth.

It was the last main line railway built in the UK prior to the opening of HS1, the Channel Tunnel rail link.

The new line also served Henley-in-Arden, making redundant the original GWR branch from Rowington Junction to Henley, which consequently closed to passengers in 1915.

The North Warwickshire Line came into operation from 1908, but the GWR's major depot in the area was at Wolverhampton (Stafford Road), and so it needed a facility to the south of Birmingham city centre.

Its existing locomotive depot at Bordesley was too small, and so land was acquired to build a Churchward-style twin-turntable layout depot, allowing for extension towards the Warwick Road for two further 65ft turntables should the need arise.

The east turntable was nominally allocated to passenger locomotives, the west to freight classes.

A standard twin-track ramped coal stage was built in between the entrance roads to the roundhouses, above which was a water softening facility, and associated water tank which stored 98,000 imperial gallons.

On the west side was a large repair depot which became known as The Factory, equipped with heavy lifting gear and full engineering facilities to repair and completely overhaul any GWR locomotive. To the east were a series of carriage sidings and maintenance sheds.

The twin 65ft turntables gave access to 28 roads each of varying length, each with an inspection pit, in total capable of accommodating up to 36 tender engines and 287 tank engines.

Most major express trains ran north and terminated or changed engines at Birmingham Snow Hill or Wolverhampton, making access to Wolverhampton (Stafford Road) easier and quicker. Hence Tyseley always played second fiddle to its major regional sister shed, its allocation mostly made up of tank engines and freight locomotives.

Allocated 72 engines on opening in 1908,

it fulfilled both local services as well as those heading south from Tyseley South Junction and Bearley to Stratford, Cheltenham, Gloucester, Bristol, South Wales and the West Country.

After nationalisation in 1948, locomotive numbers rose till by the mid-Fifties there were 100 engines allocated, a mix of former GWR, LMS and new BR Standard designs. In 1957, Diesel Multiple Units were introduced to the Birmingham area, and so a new DMU depot was developed on the extreme west of the site beyond The Factory.

In 1963 the depot was reallocated to the London Midland Region, and the same year the freight turntable and covering shed were demolished, followed in 1964 by The Factory, on top of which a new diesel repair facility was built.

The GWR roots of the depot survived until the end, with the last allocated steam locomotives being three pannier tanks that worked the Hawne Basin on the Dudley Canal from Halesowen station until 1967.

With the demise of steam on BR in the summer of 1968, the passenger roundhouse was demolished in the same year, with plans to do similar to the coal stage.

However, the shed had already come to the attention of two pioneer preservationists, Pat Whitehouse and his friend Pat Garland.

ABOVE: A view of the Birmingham suburb of Tyseley and its steam locomotive works (centre) as seen from a police helicopter. WEST MIDLANDS POLICE

The seed which grew into mighty oaks

In 1951, the Talyllyn Railway in central Wales became the first line in the world to be taken over and run by volunteers. Two of the saviours were enthusiasts Pat Whitehouse and Birmingham accountant Pat Garland. Talyllyn apart, with both the GWR and EM gauge model railways as common interests, they struck up a lifelong friendship with steam at its heart.

Pat Whitehouse presented the hugely popular and fondly remembered Railway Roundabout series for BBC TV in the late Fifties.

In the early Sixties, with Western Region steam disappearing on a daily basis, the two Pats decided to buy a tank engine of their own, and then find a railway on which to run it.

In 1961, the South Devon Railway Society was formed with the aim of saving the GWR Moretonhampstead branch as a steam line, but failed for various reasons.

At the same time, a group of businessmen, inspired by the revival of the Bluebell Railway in Sussex, and including the two Pats, focused on the region as they looked for a closed branch line to reopen as a tourist attraction. They correctly predicted that in a prime summer holiday area, the public would be willing to pay for a ride behind the otherwise extinct steam locomotives.

They also looked at the GWR South Brent to Kingsbridge branch, but despite support from local councillors, contractors began lifting the tracks almost as soon as it had closed in 1963, as was the case in the Beeching era and for many years afterwards. It was as if the powers that be were determined that closed railways would never reopen.

So the businessmen then focused their attention on the GWR Totnes to Ashburton branch, which had just closed to freight after passenger services ended on November 1, 1958. Accordingly, the Dart Valley Light Railway Company Limited was set up to buy the line and acquire suitable locomotives.

ABOVE: The now-unique outline of an A3 Pacific resplendent in the Birmingham sunshine on September 16. ROBIN JONES

Pat Whitehouse was undertaking a building job on a bridge when a chance conversation with the stationmaster at Walsall led to him and Pat Garland buying their first engine, GWR 2-6-2 tank engine No. 4555 for £700. The deal included a spare boiler, an overhaul at Swindon Works and a load of spare parts.

The two Pats then bought GWR pannier tanks No. 6435 (with enthusiast John Wilkins) and No 1638, plus Collett auto tank No. 1420 for the Dart Valley. At the time, the new heritage line was not ready to accept the locomotives, which had to be stored.

Pat Whitehouse negotiated the use of the steam depot at Tyseley in Birmingham for the purpose.

While it was based at Tyseley, as payment for its accommodation, No. 4555 returned to British Railway service, even though it was privately owned and had been repainted from British Railways livery to GWR green with appropriate lettering on the side. Tyseley's sympathetic shedmaster occasionally rostered the prairie tank for the 5.25pm commuter train from Birmingham Snow Hill to Knowle & Dorridge. That allowed Pat Garland to catch 'his' train ▶

BELOW: On each of the three mornings of its visit to Tyseley Locomotive Works, *Flying Scotsman* wowed the crowds. MICHAEL WHITEHOUSE

ABOVE: You don't have to steam on rails to get a piece of the action! This magnificent Aveling & Porter steam roller was strutting its stuff outside the entrance to Tyseley Locomotive Works during the visit of *Flying Scotsman*. ROBIN JONES

home – but not as a passenger in the accepted sense of the word. An amateur driver, he could jump on the footplate of his engine and take control of the regulator!

The privately owned No. 4555 was also used for short freight workings, carriage shunting and hand hauling 'last' specials over the Bromyard, Brecon, Wombourne and Severn Valley routes specials.

In 1967, Pat Whitehouse bought GWR 4-6-0 No. 4079 *Pendennis Castle* from another enthusiast who had purchased it following its performance on the 'Ian Allan Plymouth to Paddington special' May 9, 1964, during which its firebars had melted. However, Pat owned it for only a week before he was asked by the seller to retract his offer, as two other enthusiasts, the multi-millionaire construction company supremo Bill McAlpine and his friend

John Gretton had made a higher bid.

Pat, a gentleman with steam heritage at his heart, readily agreed, but then his attention was brought to another of the Castles on the 1964 trip, No. 7029 *Clun Castle*, which had hauled the final British Railways era steam out of Paddington on June 11, 1965.

Pat and fellow Dart Valley director John Evans made up the shortfall in a fund which had been set up to buy No. 7029, transferring the locomotive to a new company, 7029 Clun Castle Ltd. That locomotive and *Pendennis Castle* were used on specials in the first weekend of March 1967 which were arranged to mark the closure of Birmingham Snow Hill station and the GWR through route from there to Birkenhead.

However, slowly, but surely, the 1908-built Tyseley steam depot evolved a preservation

identity of its own over and above temporary storage for the Dart Valley.

In October 1968, 7029 Clun Castle Ltd bought LMS Jubilee class 4-6-0 No. 5593 *Kolhapur*, and its supporters established the Standard Gauge Steam Trust as an educational charity to preserve and demonstrate steam locomotives.

Patrick Whitehouse negotiated a lease bid, with plans to adapt it for steam locomotives. This and the fact that Birmingham City Council placed a preservation order on the turntable managed to create a strip of land inside the depot that is today Tyseley Locomotive Works.

The site became Birmingham Railway Museum and is now known as Tyseley Locomotive Works. In October 1968, two months after the end of British Rail steam haulage, Tyseley held its first of many, and very successful, enthusiasts' open days. That year, the old coaling stage was converted into a two-road shed with an inspection pit to hold both acquired locomotives. Two water columns were repaired to allow steam locomotives to stay at the site.

Fast forward to today, and Tyseley, which is not generally open to the public as a museum apart from eagerly awaited open weekends each year, is one of Britain's foremost depots for maintaining and overhauling steam locomotives for use on the main line, especially those of GWR pedigree which formed the bulk of its operational fleet. British Rail Engineering Ltd closed Isambard Kingdom Brunel's Swindon works in 1986, but Tyseley's chief mechanical engineer Bob Meanley and his team have well and truly taken on the steam era mantle that was so long held by Swindon.

Tyseley's operating arm, Vintage Trains, runs many special trains during the year, including the twice-daily summer Sunday 'Shakespeare Express' trips to Stratford, which began in 1999. It even has its own platforms with its complex, Tyseley Warwick Road, a stone's throw from Network Rail's Tyseley station, which serves the junction for the North Warwickshire Line.

Indeed, Tyseley Locomotive Works today stands proudly as a monument to the multiple ground-breaking achievements of Pat Whitehouse in those early days.

And no doubt he would have been proud to witness one of its more successful events in its heritage-era history, the visit of *Flying Scotsman*.

Taking the second city by storm without hardly moving a muscle!

While at Tyseley, *Flying Scotsman* did not haul public trains, but wowed the record crowds nonetheless.

Each day it would stand on the turntable to the delight of spectators and photographers before reversing off and running forward into the Warwick Road station platforms, where it remained for public inspection and infinitely more photographs.

There, as part of a special *Flying Scotsman* footplate experience, which was sold out within days of being announced, hundreds signed up to walk through the A3 corridor tender and visit the footplate.

Once there, they heard an explainer recount the locomotive's exploits of being the first officially to reach 100mph, in 1934, and which, after being privately bought by the late Alan Pegler in 1963, continued to operate during the 1968-71 BR steam ban and visited North America and Australia before being saved for the nation by the National Railway Museum in 2004.

GWR 4-6-0 No. 5043 *Earl of Mount Edgcumbe* also thrilled the crowds with turntable demonstrations during the weekend. Pannier tanks Nos. 9600 and L94 topped and tailed the free depot shuttle train, while Peckett No.1 shunting locomotive ran demonstration

goods trains and even the centre's Class 47 No. 47773 *The Queen Mother* made an occasional appearance, fresh from hauling a fully booked excursion to the Isle of Wight only a week before.

Visitors were able to visit the recently completed state-of-the-art European Regional Development Fund grant aid-supported locomotive workshops and, from the viewing gallery, see progress on three major repair projects: GWR 4-6-0 No. 7029 *Clun Castle*, LMS Jubilee 4-6-0 No. 45596 *Bahamas* and unique BR 8P Pacific No. 71000 *Duke of Gloucester*.

Tyseley Locomotive Works currently employs 25 people supporting its engineering services

ABOVE: History makers side by side: the year 1971 was a seminal one for steam in the UK on two counts. Firstly, while London is not generally considered to be part of the national rail network, June 6, 1971 marked the last steam on the tube. Secondly, that autumn, British Rail relaxed its three-year ban on steam haulage on the national network, which had applied to all but one locomotive, *Flying Scotsman* (although that distinction was by then purely academic as it was marooned across the Atlantic). As pannier tanks became displaced by diesels in the Fifties, and also several of the rural lines on which they provided a mainstay of service closed years before Dr Richard Beeching arrived on the scene wielding his axe, several were sold off privately into industry, and 13 were eagerly bought by London Transport to haul engineering trains on London Underground. The relationship between the Underground and the GWR had turned full circle: in 1863, when the first section of the Metropolitan Railway, the world's first underground line, opened, the GWR supplied broad gauge engines to run services. Carrying maroon London Transport, these panniers outlived steam on British Rail by three years, the last Underground pannier coming out of service on June 6, 1971, while some 57XX panniers lasted in National Coal Board ownership for several years more. After their final fires in steam era revenue-earning service were thrown out, several GWR panniers were given a new lease of life in Britain's growing portfolio of preserved railways, where they remain a familiar and popular sight to this day. No. 7752 is one of those lucky survivors, and indeed, featured on the front page of the *Daily Telegraph* as well as the 10 o'clock news on TV that day when it hauled the last Underground steam train. Built by the North British Locomotive Company Ltd in Glasgow in November 1930, it was delivered to Swindon along with No. 7760 and its first shed allocation was Aberdare. After a general repair at Swindon Works in May 1934, it was sent to Newport Ebbw Junction, and remained in that locality until 1943. From August 1943 until November 1946, it was allocated to Aberbeeg and Aberdare sheds, and then shedded or stored at Tondu for the rest of its national network career, with repairs being undertaken at Caerphilly Works. It was sold to London Transport on November 1, 1959 and became L94 on the Underground, where it worked engineering trains. Its biggest claim to fame might have been its last-ever working, and in recent times, it has proudly carried its London Transport livery at its Tyseley base. Yes, there was to be no one-way trip to a scrapyard for No. 7752. It was bought straight out of service by 7029 Clun Castle Ltd. During the visit of *Flying Scotsman*, it ran passenger shuttles in and out of the Warwick Road platforms where the A3 was parked for footplate experience sessions and general admiration. But it cheekily sent out a message to the more illustrious visitors: "I've got a place in history too!" ROBIN JONES

to Britain's heritage railways while also promoting its own tourist trains on the national railway network.

Pat Whitehouse's son Michael, who is carrying on his excellent work as chairman of Vintage Trains, said that some of the visitors to the event over the weekend of September 16-18 had never seen a steam locomotive before. He said: "Most visitors were amazed to hear that the centre's steam locomotives regularly hauled tourist trains to interesting market towns such as Stratford, Oxford, Hereford and Chester. GWR 4-6-0 No. 4965 *Rood Ashton Hall* as the locomotive hauling the summer Sunday 'Shakespeare Express' from the City to Stratford proved very popular." Especially when the commentator revealed it was 90 years old and still working as designed – and that its tender was 100 years old – the oldest item on wheels still running on Network Rail.

The main line as opposed to the heritage sector still very much has a presence at Tyseley. Next door to Tyseley Locomotive works is Tyseley traincare depot, used by train operator London Midland as a servicing point for its DMUs of Class 150 Sprinter and Class 172 Turbostar units. The depot is also used by some Arriva Crosscountry classes 170, 220 and 221 due to its convenient location near their central hub of Birmingham New Street.

ABOVE: For Swindon 1950, read Tyseley 2016! Inside the state-of-the-art workshops, preservation icon GWR 4-6-0 No. 7029 *Clun Castle* is being readied for a long-awaited return to main line service in 2017, while on the right, work is under way on the overhaul of unique BR 8P Pacific No. 71000 *Duke of Gloucester,* which, dating from 1954, represents the last design of steam locomotive for the British Railways network.

ABOVE: Back where any self-respecting A3 belongs – at the head of a train, at Warwick Road on September 16!
ROBIN JONES

ABOVE: *Flying Scotsman* reverses off the turntable at Tyseley before taking its place in the Warwick Road platforms. ROBIN JONES

ABOVE: The British Railways lion-and-wheel logo on the tender of *Flying Scotsman.* ROBIN JONES

Another classic back on the main line

As we will see in the next chapter, immediately after its starring role at Tyseley, *Flying Scotsman* made a light engine move across the West Midlands network to Kidderminster, where it transferred on to Severn Valley Railway metals.

Days later, Tyseley announced a new initiative to further boost its share of the main line tour market, by announcing a £1 million appeal to restore its long-dormant Castle, No. 5080 *Defiant,* one of 12 class members renamed after RAF aircraft by the GWR during early 1940.

Michael Whitehouse said: "*Defiant* will be welcomed into Vintage Trains' locomotive fleet with open arms and be assured of a main line future.

"No. 5080 will play a key role in Vintage Trains' strategy which is to build on its existing GWR/BR (WR) branding by offering the travelling public a Castle on all of its main line dining trains.

"The addition of *Defiant* will enable Vintage Trains to provide one of two Castles in service – No. 5043 *Earl of Mount Edgcumbe* and No. 7029 *Clun Castle* next year (2017) with a third, No. 5080, in reserve when its overhaul is completed."

The 4-6-0 which is currently on display at the Buckingham Railway Centre – and which was once driven by author Robin Jones on a steam driving session at Tyseley in 1992 – is likely to be moved back to the Midlands during the winter months.

However, Michael said that work on the Castle will not begin until £500,000 has been donated by the public. This figure represents approximately half the estimated total required to complete a heavy overhaul and in effect, the 4-6-0 will become something of a 'people's engine'. If the public's reaction proves to be less than anticipated, the overhaul will be delayed until sufficient funds are accumulated.

ABOVE: *Flying Scotsman* may have left Tyseley, but immediately the race has begun to return another classic locomotive to the main line, in the form of GWR Castle 4-6-0 No. 5080 *Defiant*. Dormant for too long, it has been spending its years in the overhaul queue as the flagship exhibition inside the Buckinghamshire Railway Centre's Rewley Road station at Quainton Road. ROBIN JONES

Tyseley has launched a 'Defiant Club' to help fund the overhaul. To join the club, enthusiasts are asked to subscribe £1000 up front or by paying £300 up front followed by 30 subsequent payments of £30 monthly by standing order.

In return members will be enrolled as trustee shareholders for life.

The £1000 donation will be paid into a designated bank account held by 7029 Clun Castle Ltd and ringfenced for *Defiant*. Any gift aid reclaimed from HM Revenue & Customs will also be paid into the same bank account which will then form the fund used to repair the 4-6-0.

7029 Clun Castle Limited will contract Tyseley Locomotive Works to repair *Defiant* to comply with Network Rail Group Standards for operation on the national network and also to Tyseley Locomotive Works' own maintenance and overhaul policy as regards quality of repair, processes and maintenance arrangements.

Anyone who would like to see *Defiant* rejoin *Flying Scotsman* on the main line are asked to contact defiant@vintagetrains.co.uk for full details. ●

BELOW: Bought from Barry scrapyard by Tyseley initially as a source of spaces for sister Castle 4-6-0 No. 7029 *Clun Castle*, No. 5043 *Earl of Mount Edgcumbe* has been rebuilt by Bob Meanley and his men into one of the finest steam performers on the main line today, and regularly heads Vintage Trains services. Built in March 1936, it was originally named *Barbury Castle*, and was renamed *Earl of Mount Edgcumbe* in September 1937. It had a double chimney and 4-row superheater fitted in October 1958. Its first shed allocation was Old Oak Common; from June 1952 to February 1956 it was based at Carmarthen, before returning again to Old Oak Common. Like all other steam locomotives based there, with the dieselisation of Cardiff Canton it was transferred to Cardiff East Dock shed in September 1962, its final allocation. It was withdrawn in December 1963, and acquired by the legendary Woodham Brothers scrapyard the following June. Sold to Tyseley, it became the 43rd departure from Barry in September 1973. Many of its parts were removed for safekeeping and the locomotive was stored, initially as a spare boiler for *Clun Castle*. However, museum trustees announced the project to restore No. 5043 to main line running condition. The proposal was to restore the locomotive to late 1950s condition, with a newly constructed Hawksworth tender and BR double chimney. In 2000, No. 5043 was moved into Tyseley Locomotive Works. While checking the inside crossheads for repair and refitting, they were found to have been fitted at one time to sister *Defiant*. Late 2007 the boiler was steamed up and approved, and the locomotive moved again under its own steam on October 3, 2008. Its first golden moment came on April 17, 2010, when it headed a commemorative train, 'The Bristolian' to mark the GWR 175th anniversary. No. 5043 hauled it non-stop from London to Bristol, and later the same day back from Bristol to London. On its return journey, arrival at Paddington was about 45 minutes early, just under one hour and 50 minutes after leaving Bristol Temple Meads. *Earl of Mount Edgcumbe's* journey time was only a few minutes longer than the schedule for the non-stop steam era 'The Bristolian' in the late Fifties, and was achieved notwithstanding the current speed limit for steam of 75mph, which did not apply in the 1950s. A source of spares indeed! At that time, *Flying Scotsman* was undergoing its protracted overhaul by the National Railway Museum. While the cat's away, the mice will play? ROBIN JONES

Chapter 10

Pacific Power

What happens when the two most popular operational locomotives in Britain run together on the country's second most popular heritage railway? A record 45,000 people turned out over six days for the Severn Valley Railway sell-out Pacific Power gala in September 2016.

ABOVE: Hauling a nine-coach rake of Gresley teak coaches, *Flying Scotsman* thunders towards Foley Park tunnel en route to Kidderminster on September 23. JOHN TITLOW

in the Valley!

The Severn Valley Railway has always done what it said on the tin. It originally ran from A to B, or Shrewsbury to Hartlebury Junction, using the contours of the slopes of the river valley and thereby minimising the cost of major engineering feats.

However, the big drawback with any cross-country routes is that not that many people want or need to travel from A to B, but for the most part, probably between only a pair of intermediate stations. Yes, such routes play an important role in shipping in and out supplies of essential commodities such as coal, and taking agricultural produce to the nearest market, but what happens when the day comes that road transport can do the same job cheaper and with greater versatility, or when households switch to a less dirty and smoky fuel?

The 40-mile Severn Valley line was built between 1858-62, and was absorbed into the GWR. A link between the intermediate stop of Bewdley and Kidderminster was built in 1878, allowing trains to run directly from the industrial Black Country into Shropshire.

In steam days, the route was never financially successful. Freight traffic, mostly agricultural, and coal traffic from the collieries of Alveley and Highley were the principal sources of revenue.

However, the line was strategically useful in World War Two as a bypass around the West Midlands.

Passenger numbers began to fall after nationalisation in 1948, and services were earmarked for withdrawal even before the publication of Dr Beeching's infamous watershed report of March 27, 1963, The Reshaping of British Railways, in which he called for the closure of one-third of the country's 7000 railway stations.

The line was closed to through passenger and freight services on September 9, 1963, and the track north of Bridgnorth was dismantled. Coal traffic survived south of Alveley until 1969, while a basic DMU passenger service continued to link Bewdley with Kidderminster and Hartlebury, until this too ceased in January 1970.

North of Bridgnorth, a short section of the original Severn Valley line continued to carry coal traffic to Ironbridge Power Station until its closure in November 2015. That section may one day become part of the Telford Steam Railway, but that is another story.

In the Sixties, a group of local enthusiasts looked at the phenomenal success of the Bluebell Railway in Sussex in resurrecting a closed line on which to run vintage steam trains, and wondered if something similar could be set up in the West Midlands.

Attention turned to the Cleobury Mortimer & Ditton Priors Light Railway which had been used by the Admiralty in latter days and which had recently closed. That line had not been designed to be used by the heavy main line locomotives that pioneer revivalist Keith Beddoes and his friends envisaged, and instead they looked to a line which ran parallel to the east, one with stunning riverside scenery that would be a far better proposition.

A notice was placed in the local press inviting interested members of the public to a meeting at the Coopers Arms in the Kidderminster suburb of Habberley. It would be up to those in attendance to vote on which line should be saved, if possible.

A total of 50 people turned up, and chose the Severn Valley line, at the same time forming a society to buy and reopen as much of it as possible for steam trains.

Their initial target would be the four miles of line from Bridgnorth to Hampton Loade to be reopened, plus the track from Hampton Loade to Alveley Colliery sidings, from where coal trains were still being run south to Bewdley, and which would give the nascent heritage line a connection with the national network.

Decades later, Keith recalled: "At the time it was just a dream. The way I look back at it now was that we just wanted to play trains. It was only when businessmen and the local MP became involved that we saw we could get to Bewdley and even beyond. Four miles would have been adequate – but that little spark was there and all this has happened."

WHEN ONE CALL TURNED THE TIDE OF HISTORY

Among those in attendance at that pivotal meeting was John Garth, who owned a family firm in Lye which manufactured nuts and washers. He was to play a key role.

Having decided to bid for a lease on the Bridgnorth to Hampton Loade section, the revivalists decided several days later to walk the track. Not only was July 11 a very wet Sunday afternoon, but when they reached Bridgnorth, they were aghast: the contractors had resumed tracklifting.

An emergency committee meeting was convened for that evening, following which John Garth sent a telegram to British Railways pleading for a breathing space, and promising to call the following day. He did so at 9am, and pleaded for the ripping-up of the track to be suspended.

It turned out to be the most important telephone call in the history of the modern-day Severn Valley Railway, for John found a very sympathetic ear in Phil Coutanche, planning engineer at the

BELOW: Look – no smoke deflectors! Visiting LNER A3 Pacific No. 4472 *Flying Scotsman* emerges from Foley Park tunnel during an earlier visit on October 14, 1990. BRIAN SHARPE

Wolverhampton District Engineers' Department office in Wolverhampton (Low Level) station, who was in charge of the permanent way gang lifting the track.

Phil, an enthusiast himself, lived at Linley station on the northern section of the Severn Valley line that had by then been lifted, and in his spare time, lined out models for the former Clapham Museum. He had also written books on the carriages of the South Eastern & Chatham Railway.

Phil agreed for the contractors to leave off pending further talks, tidying up what they had done at the northern end of Bridgnorth station.

Initial efforts by the revivalists succeeded in raising 25% of the £25,000 purchase price for the closed five-mile section from Bridgnorth south to Alveley.

By 1967 the first rolling stock, an engine and four coaches, had arrived at Bridgnorth, and the next three years were spent restoring the line to operating condition and in obtaining the legal powers, a Light Railway Order, from the Department of the Environment.

The section from Bridgnorth to Hampton Loade was opened for public passenger services on May 23, 1970, with GWR Colett 0-6-0 No. 3205, now based on the South Devon Railway, hauling the historic first train out of Bridgnorth. The balance of the £25,000 purchase price was paid shortly afterwards.

Following the closure of Alveley Colliery in 1969, and the ending of Bewdley passenger services in 1970, a plan was formed to raise a further £110,000 for the purchase of more of the route, spearheaded by the late Tory MP Sir Gerald Nabarro, and the fundraising was a major success.

The line was reopened, at first to Highley in April 1974, and one month later to Bewdley.

ABOVE: *Flying Scotsman* receives admiring glances from the handful of people on Bridgnorth station platform on October 13, 1990, during the Severn Valley Railway's autumn diesel gala. ARRIFLEX 2007*

A total of £74,000 was subsequently spent on purchasing the railway from Alveley through Bewdley to Foley Park, near Kidderminster, where a connection with the main line was made. The two-mile section of line from Bewdley to Foley Park, although purchased in 1974, was, for a decade, only used on special occasions, mainly by steam trains during Enthusiast Weekends.

This section of the line was also used by diesel multiple units from the mainline on peak Saturdays and bank holidays, and by diesel locomotive hauled excursions.

The British Sugar Corporation sidings at Foley Park became disused in 1982, and in 1983-84, more than £370,000 was raised by an SVR share issue, £80,000 of which was used to buy the line between Foley Park and Kidderminster Junction. The asking price was a whopping £450,000.

Bridging finance was agreed with the company's bankers prior to the successful launch of a share offer. By then, the railway had grown in support and stature to the extent that not only was the asking price raised but the share issue left money to spare.

Chairman Michael York commented in the final paragraph of his letter to prospective shareholders: "It is vital to secure outright ownership of the entire railway from buffer stop to buffer stop."

The balance of the money raised from the SVR share issue was used to develop the former railway goods yard site in Comberton Hill, Kidderminster, to form a new passenger station, which become known as Kidderminster Town.

The new section from Bewdley to Kidderminster Town was opened to passenger services on July 30, 1984, and so was completed the fantastic 16-mile route from Kidderminster to Bridgnorth which is so beloved by families from the Birmingham/Solihull and Black Country conurbation. The railway today carries up to 250,000 passengers a year, and in terms of ticket sales, is second only to the North Yorkshire Moors Railway.

THE NEW VICTORIAN TERMINUS

First-time visitors to red-brick Kidderminster Town station would never guess that it has not 'always been there' and is a survivor from the steam age. Yet everything that you see here is new.

Its Victorian design is based on a turn-of-the-century GWR design for Ross-on-Wye, and the station's final wing was completed in 2006, together with a canopy covering the station concourse. The design of the steelwork for this canopy has been closely based on the former GWR Wolverhampton Low Level station.

In 2000, the carriage shed was constructed within the Kidderminster Town site. A fifth of a mile long, it is the UK's largest on a heritage railway with a capacity of 56 bogie vehicles – including the priceless rake of teak coaches which have been restored on the Severn Valley Railway…and which would look particularly marvellous behind a visitor LNER-design locomotive, such as an A3 or an A1…

The Severn Valley route was never designed for big heavy locomotives like Pacifics, and for most of its steam era existence, tank engines and smaller tender locomotives formed the mainstay of its traction.

However, the heritage era railway is a very different animal indeed. Yes, you would not normally have seen mighty Pacifics hauling sizeable trains on a single-track cross-country route, but in the preservation era, the blend of stupendous scenery and the presentation of immaculately restored engines and locomotives works to resounding success – another major chapter if not a whole volume to itself in the story of the romance of the railways.

The immense value of the railway to the local economy became only too evident in 2007 when it was decimated by two freak midsummer floods.

On the night of June 19, and coincidentally exactly a month later on July 19, heavy rain fell on already saturated ground, causing major damage to the line in no fewer than 45 separate locations, leaving the line out of action north of Bewdley.

At 10 of these locations the damage was so serious that major engineering solutions had to be found before reconstruction could commence. A flood damage disaster appeal was launched which raised more than £500,000 which, together with further help from the Heritage Lottery Fund and the European Regional Development Fund, provided most of the finance for what turned out to be a £3.5 million repair bill. The repairs took nine months to complete.

However, the following year, another major attraction was opened on the line in the form of the Engine House museum and visitor centre at Highley station.

Not only has this provided another big visitor draw and splendid educational facilities, but has allowed out-of-ticket locomotives and wagons to be stored under cover, protecting them from ▶

ABOVE: *Tornado* passes by some early autumn colours at Highley on September 24, 2011. 70023VENUS 2009*

BELOW: *Tornado* sweeps along at Blackstone on the 9.14am Bridgnorth-Kidderminster service on September 22. HUGH LLEWELLYN*

deterioration by being left outside in all weathers. Again, it was part-financed by the Heritage Lottery Fund and the European Regional Development Fund, together with Advantage West Midlands.

The opening of the Engine House was delayed for a year by the flood damage. It was officially opened by the Duke of Gloucester in October 2009.

Despite its success, which has gone way beyond anything that the original revivalists ever dreamed possible, the railway is not content to rest on its laurels, but is forever seeking ways of boosting the quality of the visitor experience in order to keep up with a market that forever demands higher standards.

On November 1, 2016, the railway launched a share issue solely to raise funds for its £5 million redevelopment of Bridgnorth station – the most significant project in the railway's 51-year history after Shropshire County Council gave the project the green light weeks earlier.

The railway's Bridgnorth Development Project Team had spent years on extensive internal and external consultations, planning, surveys, assessments and research to compile the project application.

The three-phase project will dramatically improve facilities at Bridgnorth, improve visitor facilities and provide a fitting gateway both to the heritage line and the town of Bridgnorth – where traders were badly hit when the line remained closed after the floods of 2007.

The railway has now begun a mammoth fundraising campaign in earnest to fulfil the plans of phase one and phase two.

Phase one of the redevelopment will consist of two projects – the first, the construction of a GWR c1900-style single-storey building to the south of the existing Bridgnorth station building, housing a traditional tea/refreshment room. New toilet facilities will also be housed within this building. Physical work starts on the new building in October.

The second project will focus on the conservation of a unique piece of railway history as the listed station building will undergo repairs and sensitive improvement. The works package will include an extension of the bar and seating area in the Railwayman's Arms public house, the relocation and renewal of retail and heritage areas, a new disabled toilet and the restoration of the 150-year-old booking hall, returning it to its former glory.

SVR general manager Nick Ralls said: "It is very fitting that, just having celebrated its 50th anniversary, the SVR could be embarking on such a groundbreaking project that promises to not only secure its future as one of the region's stand-out visitor attractions, but to also continue its significant contribution to the local economy for the next 50 years and beyond."

The station site also includes a Scheduled Ancient Monument. The SVR has worked closely alongside Historic England to ensure that Pan Pudding Hill, a 12th-century siegework overlooking the railway at the southern end of the station, is rightfully preserved and the heritage of the site as a whole is enhanced.

Raw power breaks the records

ABOVE: *Flying Scotsman* runs round its train at Bridgnorth on September 21, having pulled the first VIP special of the day from Kidderminster tender first. ROBIN JONES

ABOVE: Spectators vie for position on the Bridgnorth station footbridge to watch *Flying Scotsman* depart with the return VIP special to Kidderminster on September 21. ROBIN JONES

One of the – if not *the* – biggest events of the Severn Valley Railway's 51-year heritage era history was Pacific Power, which was held over September 21-26, 2016, with *Flying Scotsman* and *Tornado* topping the bill.

The one-off event replaced the line's hugely popular traditional autumn gala, for one year only. When the possibility of both engines being available at the same time arose, it became clear that special measures would need to be taken to cope with the far bigger than normal crowds, if the public response to both locomotives, especially in view of the *Flying Scotsman* trespass incidents, was anything to go by.

Both *Flying Scotsman* and *Tornado* had, of course, visited the line before, but there had never been a time when they were there together.

Flying Scotsman visited in 1990, and *Tornado* attended the autumn steam gala in October 2009, during its first year of operation, and returned again in September 2011.

This time round, the pair would run a series of separate trains in their own right, some appropriately comprising the line's LNER teak set, backed up by other members of the home fleet including two Bulleid Pacifics Battle of Britain No. 34053 *Sir Keith Park* and West Country No. 34027 *Taw Valley*, both of which share some DNA with *Flying Scotsman*.

For their designer, Oliver Vaughan Snell Bulleid, had both learned and contributed much as assistant to Gresley prior to his appointment as chief mechanical engineer with the Southern Railway in 1937, a job he kept until nationalisation.

In December 1912, Bulleid had rejoined the Great Northern Railway as personal assistant to Gresley, who by then had become the company's CME.

During the First World War, Bulleid joined the Army and was assigned to the rail transport arm, rising to the rank of major. After the war, Bulleid returned to the GNR as the manager of the wagon and carriage works.

Afer the Grouping of 1923 and Gresley's appointment as the CME of the new LNER, he brought Bulleid back to Doncaster to be his assistant. During this period, Gresley produced the majority of his famous locomotives and innovations, and Bulleid had a hand in many of them, including the P1 2-8-2, the U1 2-8-0+0-8-2 Garratt freight locomotive, the P2 2-8-2 and the A4.

In 1937, Bulleid accepted the post of CME of the Southern Railway at an annual salary of £3000, after Richard Maunsell retired.

In 1938, Bulleid gained approval to build the Merchant Navy class of modern 4-6-2 Pacifics, undoubtedly inspired by Gresley but also drawing on his experiences from across Europe and with all the most modern equipment: a partially welded boiler and firebox rather than traditional riveted designs, thermic syphons and a high-pressure boiler. It also included chain-driven valve-gear immersed in an oil bath, a feature that was controversial and later caused problems if not maintained properly.

The Merchant Navies were followed by the similar light Pacifics.

Immediately after its appearance at Tyseley Locomotive Works, *Flying Scotsman* and its support coach travelled to the Severn Valley, to be stabled at Bewdley.

ABOVE: The now-obligatory Scottish piper welcomes passengers on to the first train of the day hauled by *Flying Scotsman* from Bridgnorth on September 21. ROBIN JONES

ABOVE: *Flying Scotsman* departs from Bridgnorth with its first southbound train of Wednesday, September 21, one of three Severn Valley Railway Charitable Trust specials. ROBIN JONES

ABOVE: Enveloped by its own steam, *Tornado* moves off for its first turn of duty on September 21. ROBIN JONES

ABOVE: *Flying Scotsman* coasts to take its place at the front of its train at Bridgnorth. ROBIN JONES

Correctly anticipating the hordes of admirers who would turn up, largely from the neighbouring Black Country and Birmingham/Solihull conurbation, arrangements were made with local landowners for fields to be opened as car parks for a fee, and adjacent attractions such as Arley Arboretum also laid on viewing spaces, again for an admission charge.

Station platforms were made all-ticket for safety reasons, and some roads leading to stations were closed off for the event.

Tickets for trains hauled by the Pacific pair had sold out within days of going on sale, faster than if they had been for a Rolling Stones concert, and even when a small batch was added late in the day, they were snapped up within seconds.

The sheer volume of visitor information provided on the line's www.svr.co.uk website following months of meticulous planning for the event by SVR officials and its marketing and communications team, superbly led by Claire Gibbard, was widely praised at the lineside and on the station platforms by both enthusiast visitors and ordinary members of the public alike. It went a very long way to avoiding the dreaded clogged winding valley lines, arguments between motorists and trespassing on farmers' fields.

Wednesday, September 21, saw *Flying Scotsman* haul three exclusive VIP trains for members of the Severn Valley Railway Charitable Trust and their guests, while an intensive service timetable featuring *Tornado* and other locomotives operated.

It was the first occasion since 1964 on which *Flying Scotsman* hauled a full rake of nine Gresley-designed teak carriages.

Many trust members and friends who travelled on the specials dressed up in 1930s attire for the occasion.

The trust also welcomed two film crews, two radio stations and dozens of regional and heritage reporters and photographers. At a stroke, the event generated an enormous amount of publicity for the railway, and helped reinforce its profile as a major heritage attraction.

The event received coverage on ITV Central and BBC Midlands Today, which broadcast its programme live from Bridgnorth station, fuelling interest for the main public days which followed.

Few of the hundreds of thousands of annual visitors to the Severn Valley Railway realise the scale of the costs involved in keeping such a magnificent railway operating.

While its day-to-day operation is covered by ticket sales and the profits from catering and retail outlets, the railway needs substantial additional funding to restore and maintain both its infrastructure and rolling stock.

Unless these investments are made, over time, piece by piece, the whole railway would grind to a halt. You don't need Beeching to tell you that.

To make sure that such a scenario like this never happens, the SVR Charitable Trust was established in 2012. It has already made substantial contributions towards various projects on the railway such as the launch and ongoing operation of the Heritage Skills Training Academy, track relaying, and the building of a brand new diesel depot at Kidderminster, a major first for a UK heritage line.

Furthermore, the trust has taken on ownership in perpetuity of various pieces of rolling stock, including GWR 4-6-0 No. 7819 *Hinton Manor* (currently awaiting restoration) and numerous carriages and wagons.

Most notably, the trust owns the only complete restored set of nine Gresley-designed teak carriages in existence, and these came into their own like never before during Pacific Power. The restoration work on one of these, Kitchen Composite No. 7960, was brought to completion thanks to the trust's intervention, building on decades of dedicated work and investment by volunteers.

There's still so much more work for the trust to do. For example, £1 million is needed to restore the beautiful seven-arched Falling Sands viaduct, so that speed restrictions for trains can be avoided, as well as damage to locomotive and carriage springs. The trust also makes substantial contributions towards the railway's annual £600,000 bill for locomotive overhaul.

ABOVE: Among the tens of thousands of lineside observers during *Flying Scotsman's* visit to the Severn Valley were this family of African elephants at the West Midlands Safari Park near Bewdley. Two-year-old Sutton, his mother Five and his aunt Latabe, aged 23 were grazing in their enclosure which is next to the line when the locomotive went past on September 21. Lewis Hodson, deputy head of elephants at the park, said: "The elephants have grown up with the sights, smells and sounds of the trains going past on the Severn Valley Railway and it has always been a nice backdrop to their enclosure." The safari park, like the railway which runs alongside, is a hugely popular day trip destination for West Midlands families. The park was opened by Jimmy Chipperfield on April 17, 1973 and at the time hosted a few former circus animals. It now holds more than 165 species of exotic animals, with other attractions including a small theme park. The park contains the largest groups of white lions, cheetahs, hippopotami and meerkats in the UK, as well as the largest lemur walk-through exhibit. The park was the first safari park in Britain to have all five African so-called 'big game' animals, although its leopards have since been moved to Scotland, leaving it with only four of the five. West Midlands Safari Park is well known for its efforts in conservation. The park contains many animals that are on the International Union for Conservation of Nature's endangered or critically endangered list. In May 2014, the park's dedicated Elephant Valley became home to Sutton, the first male African elephant successfully born in the UK, and now an inadvertent linesider! Will he ever forget to bring his camera or a spare SD card on gala days, I wonder? WEST MIDLANDS SAFARI PARK

ABOVE: *Flying Scotsman* heads its teak train through Bewdley South Junction en route to Kidderminster on September 23. DUNCAN LANGTREE

LEFT: All prepared and raring to go: while *Flying Scotsman* was backing on to its first train of the day from Bridgnorth on September 21, *Tornado* was waiting in the wings outside Bridgnorth shed all ready for the next service to Kidderminster. ROBIN JONES

ABOVE: Having arrived on the line several days before *Flying Scotsman*, *Tornado* drifts over the landmark Victoria Bridge across the River Severn with a service train on September 8. JOHN TITLOW

ABOVE: *Flying Scotsman* passes Trimpley Reservoir on September 21. JED BENNETT

ABOVE: Pride of Britain: the boys in blue took turns in having their pictures taken in front of green giant *Flying Scotsman* at Kidderminster Town station after it arrived through a downpour late on the afternoon on September 21. It takes more than a shower to deter the strong arm of the law! ROBIN JONES

ABOVE: *Tornado* runs towards Northwood Lane, past the point where the GWR line from Bewdley through the Wyre Forest to Tenbury Wells and Woofferton diverged from the Bridgnorth line. The pillars of the bridge which carried the line over the River Severn can still be seen. ROBIN JONES

BELOW: Clear road ahead: in a whirlwind of steam, *Tornado* departs Highley bound for Bewdley and Bridgnorth on September 21. ROBIN JONES

ABOVE RIGHT: Watercolour artist and Severn Valley Railway Charitable Trust volunteer Alan Reade created Art Deco-style images of the Pacific and signed limited edition prints were handed to each passenger on the VIP charity specials on September 21. The pictures are available to purchase in a range of forms including SVR-related prints, notelets and calendars from Alan's stall on special event days. Alan, who lives in Claverley, Shropshire, said: "This is the third series of posters I've done. The first lot I did in 2009 and I made a calendar out of those for 2013 after selling them as prints. Then I did another set in an Art Deco style, and I made those into a calendar as well for the SVR Charitable Trust. This year, because of the visit of the *Flying Scotsman* and *Tornado* which has caused quite a bit of a stir, I did a picture of the *Flying Scotsman* and *Tornado* and two GWR engines, Hagley Hall and Hinton Manor." Copies of his calendar featuring *Flying Scotsman* and *Tornado* can be obtained from Smith York Fine Art Publishing Limited at www.syfap.net priced £5 each. ROBIN JONES

BELOW: Every seat taken: *Tornado* enters Highley with a train from Bridgnorth on September 21. ROBIN JONES

The public descends

The full-blown Pacific Power public event opened the following day, and ran until Monday, September 26.

More than 15,000 travelling tickets were sold and an estimated 30,000 additional spectators turned up over just a six-day period.

Sunny weather for days four and five of the public Pacific Power event brought spectators out in force as staff and volunteers at the railway worked around the clock to ensure the safety of passengers and spectators along the length of the line.

Amid valid concerns for the potential for trespass on the 16-mile line due to *Scotsman's* popularity and consequent disruptions to the extremely intensive timetable, stringent protocols and safety procedures were mapped out and rehearsed prior to the event.

Around 25 Severn Valley staff worked trackside over the public six-day period in 12-hour shifts to avert trespass.

Crucial to the railway's trespass management strategy was the local media's co-operation in informing the public of the dangers of trespass, building on the material publicised by diverting them to dedicated viewing opportunities provided by supportive local landowners.

Forward planning paid off as no trespass halted trains and the railway's incident book remained blank as the couple of very minor potential trespass situations were swiftly dealt with by diligent lineside teams.

In one incident, a frustrated photographer who literally saw red when a nine-year-old boy stood between him and a clear view of *Flying Scotsman* was cautioned by police.

The boy, wearing a bright red pullover, appeared at the nature reserve in Stourport Road, Bewdley, just as the green A3 was due to go past. It was understood that several other photographers were at the location at the time.

Witnesses said that after arguing with the boy, the photographer attempted to move him.

It was understood that the boy immediately went home and told his parents, who called police.

A police spokesman said: "West Mercia Police received reports of an assault at around 1pm on Friday, September 23.

"A 73-year-old man from Redditch received a caution following the incident, in which he is believed to have used force to move a nine-year-old boy out of his way while he was attempting to photograph *Flying Scotsman*."

However, SVR marketing and communications manager Clare Gibbard said: "The whole event has been an incredible feat of organisation by both the staff and incredible volunteers.

"Everyone here has worked so hard for so many months and the fact that the event has gone so smoothly, in spite of unprecedented visitor numbers, is testament to the team's meticulous planning, diligence and dedication.

"We're delighted we've brought so much joy to so many people these last few

ABOVE: Not letting the LNER have it all its own way on a classic GWR cross-county route, 4-6-0 No. 7812 *Erlestoke Manor* from the home fleet powers past Northwood Lane towards Arley. ROBIN JONES

LEFT: Top of the range: the shop at Bridgnorth station, like those at the Engine House museum and Kidderminster station, had shelves packed with *Flying Scotsman* souvenirs on show. ROBIN JONES

BELOW: Even a rainstorm cannot dampen the glamour of *Flying Scotsman* as it ploughs through the downpour to Bewdley on the afternoon of September 21. ROBIN JONES

ABOVE: Determined not to be outdone by the Pacific pair of the moment, home-based Bulleid 4-6-2 No. 34027 shows its mettle as it approaches Northwood Lane on September 21. ROBIN JONES

days and it has been worth the significant investment we made to bring *Scotsman* to the Severn Valley. It was smiles all the way along the line for the whole six days and the *'Scotsman'* effect was particularly

powerful – we'd like to think that we've gone some way to inspiring a whole new generation of steam enthusiasts.

"We'd also like to thank our extremely co-operative landowners along the line who've

opened up their fields and farms as viewing points for spectators. The public too, who turned up in their thousands to see these amazing locomotives and donated many thousands of pounds to station funds."

BELOW: It was not just the Pacific pair and other operational locomotives that took centre stage during the Pacific Power event. The Engine House museum and education centre at Highley received a steady amount of visitors during the event. Taking centre stage there was the Severn Valley's great old soldier, Stanier 8F No. 48773, decked out in military colours. It was saved from the scrapyard by the Stanier 8F Locomotive Society, started as the 8F Preservation Society at the end of British Rail main line steam in 1968, intending to preserve a member of the class. Built in 1940 by the North British Locomotive Company in Glasgow to serve the War Department, and earmarked for service in France, when that country fell to the Nazis, No. 8233, then WD No. 307, joined sister locomotives on the LMS. By December 1941, LMS No. 8233 had been requisitioned by the WD and sent to Iran. It became No. 41.109 of the Iranian State Railways and headed supply trains to the USSR. On one occasion, it struck a camel in the Iranian desert. In 1944, it was converted to oil burning, and two years later was transferred overland to the Suez Canal Zone. It returned to the UK in 1952 for overhaul at Derby Works. Two years later it went to the Longmoor Military Railway as WD No. 500. In 1957, it returned to the main line in British Railways service as No. 48773, based at Polmadie depot in Glasgow. There, it was withdrawn twice and reinstated twice: its final allocation was Rose Grove shed in 1968, two years after receiving a heavy intermediate repair and overhauled boiler at Crewe Works. Moves to save No. 48773 were sparked when a letter from enthusiast Bill Murray to the *Northwich Guardian* in 1968 was published. *The Daily Telegraph* subsequently

highlighted the bid to buy No. 48773 for £3000 and the nationwide publicity helped raised the amount. No. 48773 headed the Locomotive Club of Great Britain's 'Farewell to Steam Special' on August 4, 1968, and afterwards it passed into the ownership of the 8F Society. Taken to the Severn Valley Railway for restoration, it featured in the first weekend of public running of the heritage line, May 23-24, 1970, running packed trains between Bridgnorth and Hampton Loade. Because it is a locomotive with a unique military history, No. 48773 has been dedicated as a memorial to the railwaymen of the Corps of Royal Engineers (Transportation) who lost their lives in the Second World War. In 1986, a service of dedication was held at Highley, led by the Dean of Hereford, and conducted with full military honours. In 2002, the society compiled a roll of honour and books of remembrance commemorating 354 known casualties. It was dedicated by the Chief Royal Engineer, Lieutenant-General Sir Scott Grant KCB, at a service held at Kidderminster Town station. Recently the names of a further 54 Second World War casualties have been identified and an additional roll of honour was produced by the society. It was unveiled by Brigadier Mike Stephens at a ceremony at the Engine House in 2011, together with a roll of honour commemorating the six railway sappers killed in an accident on the Longmoor Military Railway in 1956. In 2014, during a routine review of locomotive mileages at the Severn Valley, it was found that No. 48773 topped the mileage charters of the line, in records dating back to 1968. The 8F had clocked up 151,805 miles during the heritage era, not just on the Severn Valley but also on main line charters. ROBIN JONES

ABOVE: *Flying Scotsman* rests at Kidderminster Town after returning from Bridgnorth with the last of the three VIP charity specials on Wednesday, September 21. JAMES CORBEN

Following in *Tornado's* footsteps

Visitors to Bridgnorth station during Pacific Power were able to see first hand one of the next generation of new-build locomotives to follow in the wake of *Tornado*.

While *Tornado* was built for no-holds-barred main line action, with the occasional visit to a 25mph speed limit heritage line like the Severn Valley thrown in for good measure, it would be unlikely to prove cost-effective as a general-purpose locomotive for everyday services on a preserved railway.

What many have come to see as the ideal locomotive for the average eight-mile heritage railway is another extinct type, the British Railways Robert Riddles Standard 3MT 2-6-2T.

A project to build has its roots in a chance telephone conversation between author and future *Heritage Railway* magazine editor Robin Jones and South Devon Railway fireman John Besley in 1998.

The BR Standard Class 3 2-6-2T was a hybrid design, the chassis being closely based on and sharing a number of parts with the LMS Ivatt Class 4, and having a boiler derived from a GWR No.2 boiler as fitted to the GWR large prairie 2-6-2T and 56XX 0-6-2T.

The design and construction took place at the ex-GWR Swindon Works, along with the 2-6-0 tender engine version of the class, the 77XX.

Although the boiler shared flanged plates with the GWR No.2 boiler, the barrel was shortened by 5^{13}/$_{16}$ins and a dome was added.

In common with several other BR Standard Classes, the chassis design used a number of LMS-designed components including brake hanger brackets, flexible stretcher brackets and reversing shaft brackets. The LMS 'roots' of many of the Standard classes showed Riddles' very strong influence.

Although the chassis had many almost identical parts to the LMS Ivatt Class 4, the motion brackets were derived from the design of those fitted to the LMS Ivatt Class 2 2-6-0 and LMS Ivatt Class 2 2-6-2T.

A total of 45 Standard 3 tanks were built between April 1952 and August 1955. From new, they were based on the Western, Southern, North Eastern and London Midland regions.

Excellent locomotives, with a design lifespan of 40 years, time was not on their side. In 1955, British Railways published its Modernisation Plan calling for the eradication of steam.

So the class had a short life as most of the work that they had been built for soon disappeared with the branch lines, the closure of which had begun several years before Beeching, and the introduction of diesel multiples on shorter routes.

The last two Standard 3 tanks in service were Nos. 82019 and 82029 at Nine Elms but four more survived until after the end of steam – but not long enough for the nascent preservation movement to acquire one of them. Nos. 82000, 82003, 82031 and 82034 were transferred from North Elms at the end of 1966 to Patricroft shed in Manchester for use on local suburban trains, amd stayed until the shed's closure two years later. All four went for scrap at Cashmore's yard in Newport, South Wales and were broken up in October 1968.

John Besley's infant scheme was subsequently taken under the stewardship of Severn Valley Railway enginemen Tony Massau and Chris Proudfoot in the hot summer of 2003.

In those pre-*Tornado* days, it looked for a few years as if 82045 might prove to be just another pipe dream – and not a particularly glamorous one at that!

It took off in the late autumn of 2008 when the finished frame plates for the new engine

BELOW: *Tornado* was not the only complete and operational new-build locomotive on the Severn Valley Railway during Pacific Power, although if you blinked you might have missed the other one. Parked alongside Bridgnorth Works was the replica of Richard Trevithick's Catch-Me-Who-Can, which hauled a carriage around a train set-like circle of track near the future site of Euston Station in London in 1808, and thereby became the first locomotive in the world to haul fare-paying passengers. An A1 or A3 it ain't, and would be totally unsuitable for any form of East Coast Main Line work! The original Catch-Me-Who-Can was built in the Hazeldine & Co foundry which was established in Bridgnorth around 1792. In 1807-8, the foundry built what was Trevithick's third rail locomotive, supervised by Northumberland engineer John Urpeth Rastrick, who had joined the company after 1806. Nothing survives either of the original locomotive or the foundry, the site of which is now mostly parkland. However, the local Trevithick 200 group was formed to celebrate the bicentenary of the building of the locomotive and built a replica wih the aid of the Severn Valley workshops, and it is now based at Bridgnorth. ROBIN JONES

were delivered to the group's site at Bridgnorth on the SVR, one of the class's BR-era stamping grounds. Since then, progress on this most practical of new-build locomotives has been rapid.

The 82045 Locomotive Fund, as the group was initially called, was reconstituted as a company limited by guarantee in April 2009 and gained charitable status in January the following year, accompanied by a change of name to The 82045 Steam Locomotive Trust. From the start its stated aim is to build the next member of the class (the BR engines finished at 82044) specifically for heritage railway use and with no plans to run on the main line, because the type would probably be deemed too small to haul trains of sufficient length to make such a venture pay.

Project engineer Tony Massau, who is also a professional engineer, had considered for many years that Standard 3 tanks would be an ideal engine for average-sized heritage lines, because of their economical size.

The South Devon Railway was commissioned to build the firebox in kit form at its Buckfastleigh works, for delivery in kit form in 2016. A quantity of copper for the inner firebox was ordered by the SVR to be stored until needed.

The plan is that it will be assembled by the SVR

and that the engine will carry on its maker's plates the proud legend Built at Bridgnorth.

The success of the trust's £300,000 boiler appeal, boosted by donations of £7000 during the Severn Valley Railway's four-day autumn 2015

steam gala after more than £200,000 was raised in 18 months, also led to an up-front payment to Black Country firm Barnshaws for rolling the boiler barrel, now to Bridgnorth. In summer 2016, work reached the stage where the two barrel sections ▶

ABOVE: For Swindon yesteryear, read Bridgnorth in the years to come: in a scene being recreated by a project team based on the line, BR Standard 3MT 2-6-2T No. 82030 is pictured outside Swindon Works on October 18, 1959. RL COOK/82045 SLT

BELOW: *Flying Scotsman* crossing Victoria Bridge on September 22. ANDY LOCK

ABOVE: Artist Alan Reade's watercolour painting of *Flying Scotsman* crossing Falling Sands viaduct. ROBIN JONES

ABOVE: The project to build a new Standard 3MT tank is historically appropriate for the Severn Valley line, for it will represent a type which was once in use on it. Long-scrapped Standard 3MT 2-6-2T No. 82009 is seen at Bridgnorth on May 27, 1959. R HAMILTON/82045 SLT

were fitted together. Bridgnorth's boiler shop will prepare the boiler barrel to receive the firebox.

In the yard outside, work progressed on the frames and the construction of the cab, fitting it to the rear bunker assembly.

The Ffestiniog Railway was booked to build the side tanks at Boston Lodge. They will be painted and lined out by the SVR volunteer team of Andy Williams and Gary Townley.

The 2016 Severn Valley Railway raffle was held in aid of No. 82045 and recorded its best-ever

result – with more than £30,000 going towards the project.

Organised by SVR veteran and 82045 Steam Locomotive Trust trustee Alvin Barker, the raffle was held to raise funds for the engine's slidebars and crossheads and was drawn at Bridgnorth on August 28. With just under £26,000 raised in raffle ticket sales plus additional donations and following an excellent response to a simultaneous appeal to SVR members and shareholders, more than £30,000 was raised.

Severn Valley Railway Association spokesman Chris Walton said: "This is an outstanding result for the 82045 Trust and reflects the great popularity of the 82045 project, which is working towards providing a most practical and useful new member of the SVR's steam fleet.

"For the SVR, it is about a support framework around which other appropriate new-builds – not necessarily locomotives – could be initiated."

It is now just a matter of time before *Tornado* has a smaller cousin. ●

BELOW: Job done! *Flying Scotsman* with its support coach crosses the River Weaver on September 28, 2016, en route from the Severn Valley Railway to a return visit to the East Lancashire Railway. ANDREW*

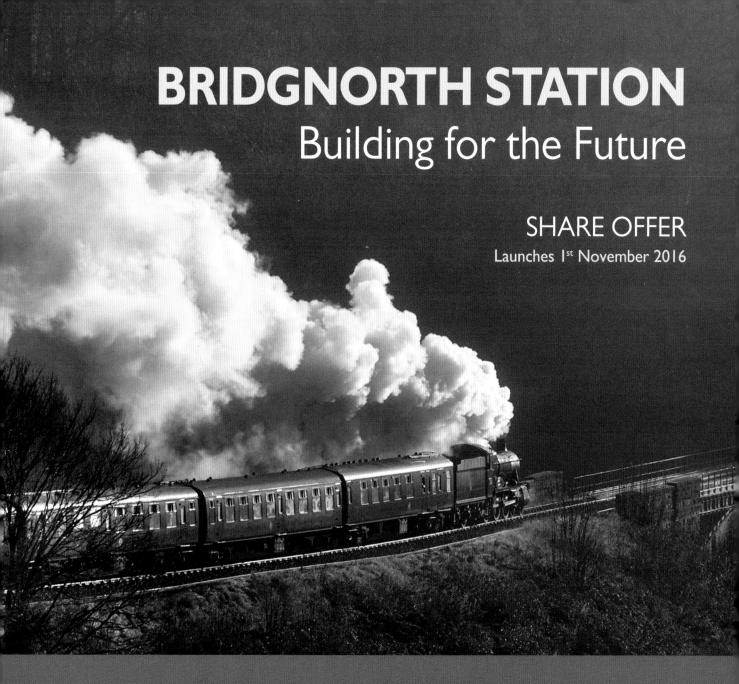

Chapter 11

Tornado at

For several years, The A1 Steam Locomotive Trust has harboured the dream of being able to regularly run *Tornado* at 90mph over the national network. However, in October 2016, it not only announced plans for trial runs at that speed in 2017, but a ground-breaking scheme to create a complete state-of-the-art charter train to run behind it.

ABOVE: *Tornado* stops at York with the return leg of the 'Scarborough Flyer' to King's Cross on June 4, 2016. ROBIN JONES **RIGHT:** *Tornado* thunders through Shere in Surrey with the Belmond British Pullman on April 8, 2016. Will the ability to travel in a steam locomotive at 90mph in a 'modern' rake of coaches rekindle the golden age of steam of the 1930s, when the LNER and LMS were locked in fierce rivalry as to which company could get from London to Scotland in the shortest time? DAVID IRELAND/A1SLT

In the heritage era, all large steam locomotives, special dispensation apart, have been limited to a maximum speed of 75mph. However, what if one could prove that it could be safely operated at higher speeds?

Provided that paths were available, in theory a major advantage would be that longer distances could be covered by charter day trips. And if that locomotive could take with it an extra water supply, eliminating the need for refilling stops, so much the better.

As we saw earlier, *Tornado* is capable of being run at 90mph, as illicitly happened without the trust's prior knowledge during its main line test runs in late 2008.

The team behind *Tornado* have for many years indicated that one day, they hope to gain permanent permission for No. 60163 to run at 90mph.

That day is now on the horizon.

At its annual convention at Darlington Locomotive Works on Saturday, October 1,

the trust announced two major new goals.

Firstly, *Tornado* was to undergo 90mph test runs in early 2017 to pave the way for its operation at such a speed on selected routes. Normal practice is that such test runs involve attaining a speed of an extra 10%, so *Tornado* would be driven at 99mph during them.

Engineering activity is now developed to enable tests, which has the full support of the trust's operator DB Cargo. Secondly, the trust announced another heritage era first: the building of a charter train using modern rather than steam-era carriages to suit the demands of a more discerning travelling public.

It is planned to use locomotive-hauled Mk.3 carriages currently in service in East Anglia for the purpose.

More than 240 trust members and covenantors at the convention were told that the yet-to-be-named new train will set new standards in a railtour market long

dominated by difficult-to-maintain 60 years or older vehicles.

As with all modern trains, it will be equipped with air conditioning, central door locking, controlled emission toilets, power at seat and persons with restricted mobility facilities. The passenger vehicles will also all be fitted with opening windows so those travelling can still experience the sound of *Tornado* working hard more clearly should they wish to do so and consideration is being given to equipping them with wi-fi.

Although the final formation of the train is yet to be determined, it will include kitchen cars to enable high-quality meals to be delivered to 250 first class dining passengers, a new support coach which will provide accommodation for the support crew and the locomotive's day-to-day spares and consumables and a service vehicle with generator and staff accommodation.

Furthermore, the train will also carry

90mph!

ABOVE: Members and covenantors of The A1 Steam Locomotive Trust at its annual convention in Darlington on October 1. A1SLT

sufficient additional water to extend *Tornado's* range to around 200 miles.

The refurbished train is expected to enter service towards the end of 2019.

The trust's operations director Graeme Bunker added: "Ever since we completed *Tornado* in 2008 we have wanted a train to accompany our locomotive which is of the same quality. "When promoting our own tours, the vehicles available to us for hire have been of insufficiently high quality and lacking in the amenities expected by today's passengers.

"Our new Mk.3-based train will at last provide what we believe passengers are looking for in a 21st-century charter train."

The convention was also told that the trust is seeking a new site in the Darlington area with larger facilities for new steam locomotive construction, maintenance, operations and education, replacing its existing base at Hopetown next to the Head of Steam Museum at North Road station.

The new site would be main line connected with the potential for a turntable and a carriage shed for the new train.

A detailed plan is close to being finalised and initial discussions have already been held with Darlington Borough Council, Network Rail and the Heritage Lottery Fund – all of whom have been supportive of the plan.

ABOVE: First class passenger: The A1 Steam Locomotive Trust's 'own' charter trips have been praised for quality and comfort, yet are restricted to steam-era Mk.1 and Mk.2 coaching sets. Having a dedicated Mk.3 rake would provide modern comforts associated with regular train travel today. ROBIN JONES

ABOVE: Could this be the livery of *Tornado's* new dedicated train? The A1 Steam Locomotive Trust's chairman Mark Allatt has repainted several Hornby 00 gauge Mk.3 coaches to show what the planned train may look like. This one is in scumbled teak finish. MARK ALLATT

ABOVE: A BR maroon version of a refurbished Mk.3 coach in 00 scale. MARK ALLATT

ABOVE: Green and cream – another option for the planned new Mk.3 train which could also be hauled by new-build P2 2-8-2 No. 2007 *Prince of Wales*. MARK ALLATT

ABOVE: The chef is hard at work in the kitchen car of a charter run by The A1 Steam Locomotive Trust. ROBIN JONES

ABOVE: An early BR carmine and cream version of a Mk.3 coach, another livery to be considered by The A1 Steam Locomotive Trust for its dedicated charter train. MARK ALLATT

A4 *Bittern* breaks the mould

Despite wishful thinking by armchair enthusiasts, there are no plans whatsoever to prepare *Tornado* for an attempt to break A4 streamlined Pacific No. 4468 *Mallard's* 126mph world speed record, set on Stoke Bank on July 3, 1938 when it snatched the crown back from Nazi Germany.

Today, in the Network Rail Group Standard published in June 2007, steam locomotives hauling passenger trains are normally limited to a maximum speed of 60mph, except for a few locos with driving wheels of 6ft 2in diameter or larger which are approved for 75mph running.

Locomotives with driving wheels below 5ft 8in diameter are normally limited to 50mph, and those below 5ft in diameter are normally limited to 35mph.

However, *Tornado* will not be the first locomotive in the heritage era to run above 90mph.

In conjunction with the National Railway Museum's award-winning Mallard 75 celebrations in 2013, in which all six surviving A4s including *Mallard* were displayed together on three occasions, sister No. 4464 *Bittern* was given special dispensation to run at 90mph on the main line.

Bittern's first test run took place during the early hours of Wednesday, May 29, 2013.

The route chosen was Southall-Reading as far as Didcot Railway Centre where the engine was turned and serviced in readiness for the train's return to Southall.

The action-packed section of the test run took place on a 15-mile stretch of Brunel's original Paddington to Bristol line between Tilehurst East Junction and Didcot East Junction.

Running at speeds in the seventies and eighties, *Bittern* touched 90mph with its eight-coach train, providing ample time and distance

ABOVE: It was claimed that West Country Pacific No. 34092 *City of Wells* very unofficially hauled the 'Blackmore Vale Express' at 94mph on July 23, 1988. It is seen passing Barford St Martin. BRIAN SHARPE

to spare before dropping the regulator and slowing for the approach to the Didcot stop.

By hitting 90mph, DB Schenker driver Don Clarke and Gresley 4-6-2 No. 4464 *Bittern* created a new official speed record for a heritage locomotive in the UK.

The key word here is 'official', for there had been reports of unofficial runs by steam locomotives in the preservation era well in excess of 75mph.

On July 23, 1988, Keighley & Worth Valley Railway-based unmodified Bulleid West Country Pacific No. 34092 *City of Wells* hauled the 'Blackmore Vale Express' between Salisbury, Yeovil Junction and Romsey. Respected recorder GAM Wood unofficially logged it at 93mph – the limit being 60mph – according to the Railway Performance Society database. Others on board the train hinted it had touched 94mph, once between Wilton and Dinton and also near Gillingham. There

has never been any official confirmation of the speed on that day.

There is anecdotal evidence of other big engines unofficially hitting high speeds, including unsubstantiated and unpublished tales of locomotives being allowed to temporarily exceed the current 75mph steam limit by traction inspectors, in order to pull away from a service train following in the path behind.

Indeed, when driver Dave Court admitted at a Mallard 75 public seminar at the National Railway Museum that he had twice driven *Tornado* at its design speed of 90mph with 14 coaches on, he also revealed that an A4, No. 60009 *Union of South Africa*, had run at an average speed of 80mph on June 15, 2004, while hauling a Steamy Affairs trip from Newcastle to York with 13 coaches on, in conjunction with the museum's Railfest 2004 event.

BELOW: So that's why they called them 'Streaks': A4 No. 4464 *Bittern heads* across Tallington crossing next to the Whistle Stop pub north of Peterborough at 4.18pm just after dusk with the 'Capital Streak' on Saturday, December 7, 2013, on its way back to King's Cross. ROBIN JONES

Did *Bittern* hit 95mph?

However, *Bittern* was to break its new record a month later, and again later in the year.

The first of the three planned specials, the 'Ebor Streak' from King's Cross to York and back, ran to schedule on June 29 – setting a new heritage-era record of 92.5mph.

However, the following two permitted high-speed runs, the 'Tyne-Tees Streak' and the 'Capital Streak', were cancelled due to Network Rail's summer fire risk steam ban. Originally dated for July 19 and then rearranged in the first instance for August 30, the second one, 'Tyne-Tees Streak' eventually ran on Thursday, December 5.

Departing Bristol Temple Meads for York behind DB Schenker Class 67 No. 67006, the 'Tyne-Tees Streak' set out for York with 10 full coaches.

It was a day when the run-Pathfinder's train was again threatened by adverse weather conditions which had reduced all service train speeds working north of York to a maximum of 50mph because of storm force winds, strong enough to rock the station's footbridge.

However, Network Rail came up trumps. Rather than postpone the train again because of the weather and the real risk of tree branches falling on to the wires, it was allowed to proceed.

The outward journey was affected by gales that severely depleted normal services and accordingly the train had to run at restricted speed.

The wind died down somewhat for the return leg, which was ambitiously scheduled to take 67 minutes for the 80.2 miles to York

at an average timetabled speed of 71.8mph.

Maximum permissible speed derogations had been granted, easing the normal 75mph to 90mph for long stretches. Apart from slowing to 75mph for a bridge restriction at Northallerton, driver Steve Hanszar, fireman Keith Murfin and traction inspector Bob Hart combined to work *Bittern* up to 90mph for long periods.

There have been very few steam-hauled start-to-stop runs from Newcastle to York. The fastest was recorded in LNER's day, in the form of a 1946 trial run with A4 No. 2512 *Silver Fox* on six coaches taking 68 minutes four seconds.

With 10 coaches grossing around 370 tonnes, *Bittern* beat that record by 66 seconds by taking 66 minutes 58 seconds, according to *The Railway Magazine's* practice and performance expert John Heaton, who was on board the trip.

Accelerating away from the permanent 85mph speed restriction at Aycliffe, its speed crept towards the magic 90mph and hit 94mph on the 1-in-220 downgrade to Parkgate Junction. Passengers spontaneously applauded as the speed peaked.

The Thirsk to Tollerton leg was run at an average of 91.2mph with a maximum of 92mph.

Bittern operator Locomotive Services Limited's general manager Richard Corser afterwards told *Heritage Railway* that the speed had peaked at 93mph.

"We sustained 90mph for some 20 miles, peaking to 92-93mph on the southbound run between Darlington and York," said The A1 Steam Locomotive Trust's operations manager Graeme Bunker, who was travelling on the trip as a guest of *Bittern's* owner Jeremy Hosking.

However, passenger John Turner, who was seated in the front passenger coach, told the magazine that he, together with others, witnessed 95mph displayed on a tablet with a GPS speedometer app and photographed the screen for posterity. It must be pointed out, however, that GPS devices have been challenged as to their accuracy.

The third of the 90mph specials, 'Capital Streak', which had originally been booked to

run on July 27, and moved to August 31, finally ran on Saturday, December 7.

Bittern hauled the train from York to King's Cross with water stops at Retford and Connington South, and was again in sparkling form, running consistently at 90mph.

The weather on the day was very different to that of the previous Thursday, as high winds had dropped and southbound services from York were back to normal.

The A4 quickly accelerated to its normal line speed and then topped the 90mph mark after Doncaster, racing towards Retford and Newark – where the 'Ebor Streak' was clocked at 92.5mph in June.

The highlight of the trips was the run over Stoke Bank, the section of track where *Flying Scotsman* reached 100mph and *Mallard* achieved its 126mph, and which is now marked by a trackside sign.

John Heaton said: "After passing Grantham at 76.5mph, speed dropped to no lower than 71.5mph on the climb to Stoke summit, this time with 11 coaches and around 405 tonnes gross.

"After a compulsory slowing at Little Bytham, *Bittern* then took the 9.2 miles from Essendine to Werrington Junction at a flying average of 91.2mph with a maximum speed of 92mph."

ABOVE: The GPS device that indicated, rightly or wrongly, that *Bittern* had reached 95mph with the 'Tyne-Tees Streak' on December 5, 2013. JOHN TURNER

The three trips showed just what historic yet well-maintained locomotives are capable of achieving, given the right circumstances.

So how about what a nearly new Pacific can do on a regular basis? The eyes of the world will be watching those *Tornado* test runs with eager anticipation.

Come what may, there will be a team of proven achievers behind the locomotive. ●

BELOW: The blue kings of speed: current UK heritage era steam speed record holder No. 4464 *Bittern* alongside sisters No. 4489 *Dominion of Canada* and all-time record holder No. 4468 *Mallard* at the Great Goodbye, the final display of all six surviving A4 streamlined Pacifics together, at the Locomotion museum in Shildon on February 21, 2014. Will *Tornado* running at 90mph herald a 1930s-style golden age of steam in the 21st century? ROBIN JONES

Chapter 12

A locomotive better than both?

In 2016, we have revelled in the sight of *Flying Scotsman*, the world's most famous steam locomotive, and the 21st-century 'Young Pretender', *Tornado* in action, both separately and together. Beauty is in the eye of the beholder, so it is left to the people to decide which is their personal favourite. However, there will soon be a new world beater, one more powerful than either, running over Britain's network, as Graham Nicholas and David Elliott explain.

ABOVE: The original P2, No. 2001 *Cock o' the North*, being turned at King's Cross on its first day in service. A1SLT

On September 16, 2010, at a star-studded, glittering reception in London's Grosvenor House hotel, The A1 Steam Locomotive Trust was presented with a special commendation in the 'project of the year' category at the annual rail industry awards. It was a highly deserved and fitting celebration of the remarkable work that had seen No. 60163 *Tornado* enter service on the nation's main line railway the year before.

In 1934, they didn't have annual awards ceremonies (at least not in the way we'd recognise them today). But if they had, there would have been only one contender for the 'locomotive of the year' category that year – the LNER's 2-8-2 express passenger locomotive No. 2001 *Cock o' the North*.

What they did have in 1934 were voracious publicity machines, none more so than the LNER. In the pre-jet age, railways were big news and at the forefront of technological developments, so when the LNER unveiled its latest creation at a formal press launch at King's Cross station on June 1, 1934 it was indeed big news.

That locomotive was a leviathan of the rails, as big and impressive as anything seen up to that point on Britain's railways. It was immediately in demand for publicity exhibitions, which were interspersed with testing and initial service running. In these trials No. 2001 showed the capabilities of the type by taking 19 coaches (total weight 650 tons) over Stoke

summit at 56.5mph on a dynamometer test run. The LNER clearly had a potential world beater on their hands.

Yet when the six members of the class settled into everyday service on their intended route (Edinburgh to Aberdeen) this early promise was never truly fulfilled. Though not everything that was said can ever be substantiated (searches of the records at Kew and the National Railway Museum provided scant information), the locomotives gained reputations variously for spreading the track and consuming prodigious quantities of coal.

Additionally, although there were no main line derailment incidents per se, there were several recorded examples of premature crank axle failures – an undesirable attribute for any locomotive!

What is known is that, with the attention of Gresley and his LNER design team turned to new streamliner trains by 1935, little if any development of the class P2 was done (other than the abandonment of the Lentz valve gear of the prototype for conventional Walschaerts) and history records that the six original class P2s had all been rebuilt as ungainly looking Pacifics by 1944 under Edward Thompson who had succeeded Nigel Gresley as chief mechanical engineer of the LNER following his untimely death in service in 1941. From that time to the present day, the enigma of the 'what might have been' Class P2 2-8-2s has endured.

BELOW: Brand new: P2 No. 2001 *Cock o' the North* outside Doncaster paint shop. A1SLT

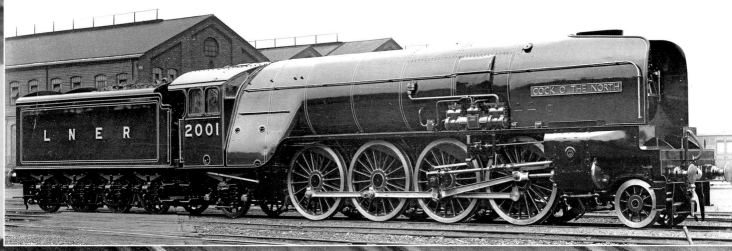

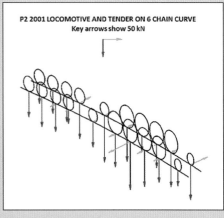

ABOVE: A diagram of P2 No. 2001 *Cock o' the North* on a six-chain radius curve. A1SLT

ABOVE: The second P2, No. 2002 *Earl Marischal*, was completed in October 1934. It was identical to No. 2001 *Cock o' the North* but with piston valves, Walschaerts/Gresley valve gear, and the ACFI feed water heater was removed. It ran a series of trials before entering regular daily service in Scotland in June 1935. In 1944, it was converted into Thompson A2/2 Pacific No. 60502, and was the only one of the class to cover more than one million miles, 360,907 as a P2 and 673,947 as an A2/2. On July 3, 1961, it became the last member of the class to be withdrawn and scrapped. A1SLT

Meanwhile what of that feted A1 project team? Basking in their glory? Resting on their laurels? No. With a credibility factor established, based on a proven formula it was a foregone conclusion that the team would wish to build a second locomotive (prosaically referred to as 'Lot 2'). The discussions revolved around ex-LNER locomotives, preferably those of Gresley origin.

In 2009, prompted by The A1 Steam Locomotive Trust, one of the railway magazines asked its readership to suggest LNER prototypes for the next new build. Out of 10 types that were put forward, approximately 60%

of all the proposals favoured a P2. This gave the team the confidence that a P2 project had 'legs'.

And what more iconic a challenge than to pick up the baton from the 1930s Gresley design team and realise the full potential of the P2 by creating the seventh member of the class – No. 2007 *Prince of Wales*.

The choice of the giant Gresley Mikado nevertheless represents a significant step forward from the work done to create *Tornado* and this is reflected in the subtle differences in the mission statement for the P2 project (compared to that for *Tornado*): "To develop, build and operate an improved Gresley class

P2 Mikado steam locomotive for main line and preserved railway use".

As a starting point for the project, the trust made good use of the years following the introduction of *Tornado* by commissioning a feasibility study into the proposed new P2. In fact, preparatory work had quietly been going on in the background for some time, even prior to the completion of *Tornado*. Central to this was work done to evaluate the ride performance of the locomotive, this being a key area to get right if permission is to be gained for operation at speed on the main line railway. Realising at an early stage that, due to the reputational issues and the limited service experience (compared to the A1), a 'grandfather rights' argument was unlikely to succeed, the trust firmly embraced modern railway design technology from the outset. Industry specialists Delta Rail were engaged to harness the power of the internationally recognised vehicle dynamics computer modelling package VAMPIRE®.

As well as being able to provide some totally fresh analysis on the issue, adoption of a computer modelling approach would considerably smooth the way to the eventual certification

BELOW: *Tornado* on a six-chain radius curve. A1SLT

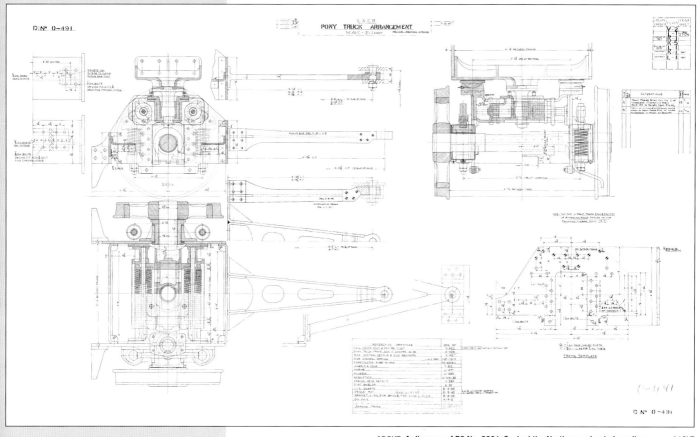

ABOVE: A diagram of P2 No. 2001 *Cock o' the North* on a six-chain radius curve. A1SLT

and approval of the locomotive, being a recognised modern-day technique to support the introduction of any new rolling stock.

A particular area for study has been the original swing-link design of the leading pony truck. Although there are no known main line derailments of P2s attributed to this feature there were no less than four affecting the V2 2-6-2s as originally fitted with the same type of pony truck. There had been at least one instance of a P2 derailment on tightly curved track in a locomotive depot. The entire V2 fleet was subsequently fitted with pony trucks which had side-control springing instead.

This is where *Tornado* has been able to lend a massive helping hand. During the original commissioning programme in 2008, the A1 Trust was tasked with undertaking some track force tests as part of the approvals for the A1. Although this was unexpected and required additional effort, it was quickly realised that here was an opportunity to get some steam locomotive ride test data 'in the bank' to validate any future computer modelling assumptions. It was therefore a satisfying thought that, as it roared through the night between York and Newcastle on that memorable evening of November 18, 2008, festooned with measuring devices as part of its own testing, *Tornado* was also helping to pave the way for its future stablemate. An intimate bond between the two locomotives was thus formed.

The work has resulted in a fully validated computer model within Vampire for *Tornado*. This work has then been extrapolated to derive computer models of the P2 as originally designed and as proposed (with the side control spring bogie).

A tweak on a spring rating here, provision of increased side clearance there and the ride characteristics of the new P2 have been evaluated and optimised; so much easier – and far less heart-breaking – than the traditional (and nowadays largely frowned upon) method of 'trying it and see if it works'.

The study showed conclusively that the myths and legends that have surrounded the original locomotive type were probably just that. An improved P2 design, featuring the developments mentioned, should produce a ride performance at least as good as *Tornado*. ▶

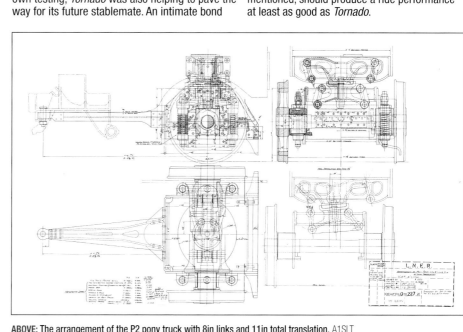

ABOVE: The arrangement of the P2 pony truck with 8in links and 11in total translation. A1SLT

Running a P2 in England

ABOVE: Scanning in drawings for the new P2 on August 23, 2012. A1SLT

Other aspects affecting the 'should we, shouldn't we?' decision were also being considered. It has always been a slightly uncomfortable truth that the particular route which influenced the original P2 design was its very undoing. The twisting, sinuous nature of the Edinburgh-Aberdeen run was by no means the kindest for an eight-coupled machine.

Among the many unanswered questions from the story of the original P2s is why they were never transferred to the southern end of the ECML during the darkest hours of World War Two when their prodigious haulage abilities would have been invaluable.

Transfer this thought forward into the 21st century, however, and this becomes the perfect raison d'être for recreating such a powerful machine.

The trust has always regarded the East Coast Main Line north from King's Cross as a 'core' route as far as it is concerned, being the spiritual home of the LNER Pacific. With modern charter train operations often dependent on the ability to fill a large train and keep to 75mph paths to minimise running times, the high performance attributes of the P2 would appear perfectly suited to the modern world.

In the meantime, as with the A1 project, it was off to the National Railway Museum to seek the drawings. This time though, the trust benefited enormously from the museum's commendable Search Engine project, implemented during the intervening 20 years since their original visits.

Although the P2 drawing collection is not as complete as those for the A1, a total of 470 drawings were scanned including the key frame and wheel drawings along with the mouth-watering General Arrangement drawing (interestingly, there never was one of these for the A1).

Overall, the output of the feasibility study was a resounding 'yes', allowing the trust to turn its attention to the formal launch of the project. Despite the undoubted success of the business model that support *Tornado*, the P2 project team led by trust chairman Mark Allatt were determined to learn lessons to ensure an even slicker approach second time around. One radical idea was the concept of a 'racing start' to capitalise on the credibility factor and show some significant early progress.

How fundraising snowballed

The idea was simple – to seek 100 people to donate £1000 by May 2014.

The response was extraordinary, with 100 people signed up in four weeks and when The Founders' Club was – reluctantly – closed in June 2014, an incredible 371 had signed up and approximately £460k (including gift aid) had been raised, largely through a series of roadshows that took the P2 project team along the East Coast route from London to Aberdeen.

Never mind 'racing'; No. 2007 was off to a meteoric start and the exercise demonstrated emphatically the obvious hunger for 'Lot 2' to be turned into reality.

A distinct difference this time though has been the adoption of a full 3D computer drawing package on David Elliott's laptop computer. With the degree of alterations to the original design that were going to be required this was an obvious application of modern technology. As well as being able to quickly and efficiently amend the physical details of the design, the program can produce elegant publicity pictures of any aspect of the locomotive, from a traditional full three-quarter view down to the tiniest minutiae of a fitted bolt, images that can easily set the pulses racing in support of the continuous fundraising activity.

Equally importantly, the 3D software knows where each component is relative to another and can easily detect when an 'impossible' juxtaposition has been proposed (something that was not so easy with the previous traditional two-dimensional drawings and which caused a few headaches with *Tornado*

ABOVE: A 3D illustration of No. 2007. A1SLT

ABOVE: The P2 team and James May with the finished article. A1SLT

RIGHT: TV presenter James May manufactured the first component of the new £5 million Gresley P2. James turned up at Darlington Locomotive Works on Thursday February 20, 2014, and made the smokebox dart, the component that keeps the smokebox door securely closed. Living up to his Top Gear nickname of Captain Slow, the celebrity spent the best part of the day patiently crafting the component at the works where *Tornado* was completed in 2008. It is estimated that it will take around 100,000 man hours to build the P2. James said: "Not many man-made machines stir the soul, but a full-blown steam locomotive is right up there, and we invented it. However, over the decades we've lost so much of the talent, skill and knowledge needed to build them. That's why it's such a thrill to work alongside the team building No. 2007 *Prince of Wales*, determined to not only resurrect this monster from the past, but to improve it using modern wizardry to do so." A1SLT

when it came down to some of the final pipe run details). Furthermore, once the details of a component are finalised, the 3D software can be easily translated into manufacturing drawings and/or linked to a supplier's computer-driven manufacturing tools, offering further efficiencies and highly accurate production of parts for the locomotive.

The opportunity has been taken to use several features already applied to *Tornado*.

The LNER under Gresley was sometimes criticised for building several small classes of specialist locomotives as opposed to large numbers of a few standard designs. However, there was much standardisation at component level, so many components which were made for *Tornado* apply to *Prince of Wales* including the whole tender, all the wheels except for the coupled wheels, most of the boiler fittings, the exhaust system and the cab side windows.

Innovations from the modern A1

The opportunity has been taken to incorporate several post-war innovations from *Tornado* including roller bearings on all axles, a hopper ash pan and rocking grate, the latter two of which greatly assist in disposing the locomotive after a run.

Several features which had been added to *Tornado* to suit modern conditions including a self-cleaning smokebox, full self-contained electrical system, air brakes and increased tender water capacity will be incorporated in the new P2.

Construction started in earnest in early 2014 when the new design was sufficiently far advanced to order the frame plates from Tata Steel (formerly Corus and British Steel) at Scunthorpe and the coupled wheel castings from William Cook Cast Products at Sheffield. Those who have followed the *Tornado* story will be aware that these are the same suppliers as for *Tornado*.

Shortly after that further castings were ordered from WCCP bringing the total number of steel castings up to 66. Many of these used patterns for *Tornado*, the major exceptions being the coupled wheels which at 6ft 2in diameter as opposed to 6ft 8in on *Tornado* required a new wood pattern. Several of the smaller castings for which no existing patterns were available have been made from expanded polystyrene patterns which have been CNC (Computer Numerically Control) machined from solid blocks of polystyrene directly from the 3D CAD models.

The frame plates were rolled at Scunthorpe on April 23, 2014 and at a small ceremony on May 21 that year, Tim and Ben Godfrey, the grandsons of Sir Nigel Gresley started

the machine to profile the frame plates.

Subsequent to this the plates were machined and drilled at Boro Foundry in Lye in the West Midlands, being one of the few ▶

ABOVE: Steel plate for the P2 frames going through the second stage rollers at Tata Steel, Scunthorpe, on April 23, 2014. A1SLT

ABOVE: The P2 frame plates arrive at Darlington on July 10, 2014. A1SLT

companies in the UK with a milling machine large enough to accommodate the 37ft-long frame plates.

Meanwhile Darlington Locomotive Works was given a thorough spring clean and various frame stands from *Tornado* construction refurbished. A "flat pack" kit of frame parts arrived on July 10, 2014. By later that day the main frames were set up on stands and construction started in earnest.

The trust can look forward to assembling the new P2 entirely within its very own facility. It is even being built the other way round this time so when the inevitable launch day comes,

Prince of Wales will be able to emerge out of its birthplace smokebox first in the traditional manner!

With much of The Founders' Club funds already committed to the frame and wheel components, further funding efforts are continuing. The ever popular covenant scheme (slogan "An A1 for the price of a pint of beer a week") used for *Tornado* has been adopted for the P2 project and already enjoys 90% of the support of the total *Tornado* take up. There is one difference though. A pint of beer is no longer £1.25 (even in the North East of England!) so it is now based on a minimum £10 per month.

ABOVE: Sir Nigel Gresley's grandsons Tim and Ben Godfrey start the profiling machine at Tata Steel on May 21, 2014.

ABOVE: The P2 frames on stands on July 11, 2014. A1SLT

ABOVE: David Champion signs up for the first covenant and the P2 covenant scheme is launched at an A1 Trust London roadshow on March 9, 2014. A1SLT

Improvements to the original design

In parallel with the start of building the locomotive, the research and design work has continued. As previously explained, the first P2 class 2001 *Cock o' the North* was fitted with Lentz rotary cam poppet valve gear. Steam locomotives were traditionally fitted with slide valves or as the 20th century moved on, piston valves to control entry of steam and exit of exhaust to and from the cylinders.

In these designs the valves work by the valve heads or pistons sliding over ports which lead to the ends of the cylinders. For poppet valves think car engine valves. These are opened and closed by a rotating camshaft. The Lentz system had been successfully applied to the LNER 4-4-0 D49 Hunt class and was chosen by Gresley for his new Mikado. The gear supplied for the new P2 was a development which used a scroll cam to enable infinite variations of cut-off as is possible with the conventional Walschearts valve gear. However, for a number of reasons mostly relating to the limits of metallurgy, it was not very successful, suffering very high rates of wear on the cams. As a consequence, Lentz reverted the gear to the earlier design with a series of stepped cams. Unfortunately, this adversely affected the economy of the engine.

David Elliott investigated the feasibility of fitting Caprotti valve gear as used on unique BR 8P Pacific No. 71000 *Duke of Gloucester* – however, the position of the middle cylinder on the P2 makes fitting it very difficult.

Research showed that during the mid-1940s, the Lentz patents were adopted by the Franklin Company in the US. Several locomotives were fitted with their version of the valve gear with infinitely variable cams and were successful in operation. However, with rapid dieselisation, the gear was never fitted to a fleet.

Unfortunately, there is no US equivalent of our National Railway Museum, so finding details and drawings was going to be a difficult task. By luck a meeting was arranged with the nonagenarian railway engineer George Carpenter (who translated French master steam locomotive engineer Andre Chapelon's seminal book La Locomotive a Vapeur into English). George had known Vernon Smith who was Franklin's senior engineer in charge of the valve gear project and who oversaw the fitment of the gear on the locomotives. He also knows Vernon's son Charles who held his father's archive. After some communication with Charles, a parcel of drawings and documents including parts and operating manuals arrived which were returned with thanks after scanning. The trust now has enough information to adapt the Franklin design for *Prince of Wales*.

ABOVE: Engineer David Elliott looking at locomotive drawing No. 3752 on January 27, 2015. A1SLT

ABOVE: The steam stand and valve castings and whistle as seen on September 28, 2016. A1SLT

Building the boiler

One of the significant areas of commonality with *Tornado* is the boiler. Although the boiler barrel of the original P2 was a little longer that the A1, that discrepancy can be compensated by a longer smokebox hidden beneath that distinctive cladding.

Seven years' operational experience with the boiler type as fitted to *Tornado* has shown it to be a prodigious steam raiser but not without some weaknesses that have meant some unplanned repairs in that time.

However, likely causes behind these issues have been identified with corresponding detailed design changes undertaken on *Tornado's* boiler (most recently during the A1's first intermediate overhaul at the beginning of 2015).

All this means that a boiler to the refined design can be ordered from Meiningen straight off the current plans. Not only will this therefore be a significantly simpler operation than with *Tornado* but the advantages of having two fully interchangeable major components are obvious. Eventually, the trust

would like to have a third boiler of the type, fully overhauled and ready to go in order to maximise the availability of both locomotives.

Tornado's boiler was funded by a £500,000 bond issue. With the outstanding success of The Founders' Club, Mark Allatt has launched The Boiler Club. This aims to attract 300 people to donate £2000 each, either as a one-off payment or as 40 monthly payments of £50 to cover the cost of the boiler and its accessories without having to borrow money. So far The Boiler Club has attracted well over 100 subscribers. ▶

Those troublesome crank axles

Meanwhile, what about those broken crank axles that beset the original P2s? In common with all Gresley three cylinder designs (but unlike *Tornado*) all three cylinders act on the same driving wheelset.

Additionally, with an increased number of driving wheels providing adhesion compared to a Pacific type, the P2s were less prone to slipping so, with the full 43,000lbs of tractive effort bearing down on this one component, particularly when starting away, its potential to be the Achilles heel is all too obvious.

Fortunately, a priceless record of one of the axle failure incidents has been unearthed (that which befell No. 2005 in July 1939 while starting away from Stonehaven with a heavy southbound train), including a crucial photograph of the fracture face.

From a study of this photograph, coupled with the details of the LNER drawing, the shortcomings of the crank axle design are all too obvious to the contemporary rail vehicle engineer, with all the benefit of hindsight that 80 years of intervening research and greater understanding of fracture mechanics can provide.

However, in order to full quantify and optimise the design, the trust engaged industry consultants Mott MacDonald to undertake a full structural analysis of the complex crank axle design, including use of state-of-the-art finite element analysis.

Following a further iteration of the design the study has confirmed that the proposed crank axle should comfortably exceed the 250,000 miles life after which the LNER and BR changed LNER type three-cylinder crank axles.

While work like the above may appear to have delayed the ordering of axle components, this is not regarded as an undue problem. The construction of the cab and smokebox has been brought forward, the latter assisted in no small part by a valuable sponsorship from a bequest to the Gresley Society Trust.

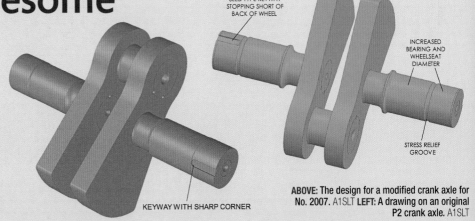

KEYWAY WITH SHARP CORNER

ABOVE: The design for a modified crank axle for No. 2007. A1SLT **LEFT:** A drawing on an original P2 crank axle. A1SLT

One lesson which the trust is determined to learn from 'Lot 1' is not to underestimate all those little detail components that are required in the final push to completion. Therefore, any slack time is being put to good use by quietly building up the necessary valves and other control fittings that will be required at the end of the project. Not only will that streamline the final run in but, with much commonality of parts, it also ensures that there are spares for *Tornado* sat on the shelf if required in the interim.

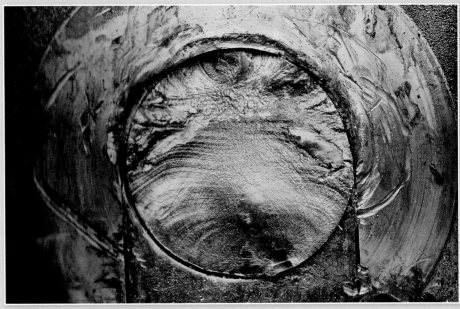

ABOVE: A 1939 photograph of the broken crank axle on P2 No. 2005. A1SLT

Looking like a P2 at last!

While the redesign continues, the locomotive continues to take shape at Darlington, with all the major frame stays and hornblocks installed in the frames. All the components for the engine wheelsets (wheels, axles, tyres, cannon and axleboxes, roller bearings and crank webs) are on hand and assembly will start shortly. However this also depends on funding.

In April 2015, supporters were asked to join the trust's latest fundraising scheme to fund the completion and installation of the wheelsets by joining The Mikado Club (to create that wheel arrangement in the UK for the first time since 1944). The target is 160 people contributing £1000 in one go or by eight monthly payments of £125. The take-up has been fantastic, at the point of writing (October 2016) there were well over 100 members.

The cab is substantially complete and the smokebox well advanced. The trust has the nameplates and the whistle!

The next major activity will be manufacture and fitting of spring and brake gear and the pony truck frame, which will enable full wheeling of the frames.

The original cylinder block on the P2 class was a one-piece (monobloc) casting incorporating all three cylinders. The problem of finding a foundry to cast something of this complexity today is considerable. However, in the latter days of steam building, the US and Germany made extensive use of fabricated steel cylinders.

The cylinders also need to be reduced in width. The original P2 design used 21in diameter cylinders which makes the cylinder block 2in wider than the cylinders on *Tornado*. The modern railway has tended to move the track closer to platforms for the laudable reason of reducing the risk of passengers falling between platforms and trains.

For steam locomotives whose cylinders are at platform height this is not good news. *Tornado* has very few platform restrictions throughout the network and it is intended that *Prince of Wales* will have similar route availability. This means cylinders no wider than those on *Tornado*. By using the full potential of *Tornado's* 250psi boiler as opposed to the original P2 boiler at 220psi, the equivalent cylinder diameter for a similar tractive effort is reduced to 19 ¾in. By using steel instead of cast iron, the thickness of the cylinder walls can be reduced, enabling the remaining ¾in to be shaved off.

Further issues with the original cylinder design were the layout of the valves for the middle cylinder with exhaust valves on one side and inlet valve on the other. Each valve needs its own port into the cylinder which makes for excessive clearance volume (the space left in the end of the cylinder, ports and valve chests when the piston is at the end of stroke) which contributes to low efficiency, as steam in that space is not able to release its energy into useful work. The present redesign is attempting to rectify this.

A further problem which will have affected efficiency was the routing of steam and exhaust passages next to each other, enabling the incoming steam to transfer heat to the outgoing exhaust before entering the cylinders. The steam and exhaust passages have been redesigned along American and French Chapelon lines to separate them.

The result is a preliminary design for a fabricated monobloc cylinder block

incorporating all these design changes – much work is still to be done before this becomes a set of manufacturing drawings!

A further successful fundraising method has been dedicated donations. Existing supporters have the opportunity to sponsor a component ranging from £25 for a driven bolt and nut up to £12,000 for a complete

wheel casting. So far this has raised in excess of £175,000.

At the time of writing P2 supporters have pledged about £2.2 million out of the anticipated £5m total build cost. While this is undoubtedly a major achievement, the rate of fundraising will need to rise significantly to meet the target completion date of end of 2021.

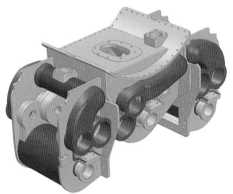

ABOVE: The CAD drawing of the new P2 cylinder block for No. 2007 with Lentz-Franklin B valves. A1SLT

ABOVE: The original monobloc for No. 2001.

ABOVE: A complete set of machined wheels at Darlington Locomotive Works on March 1, 2016.

The end in sight

With a sound pedigree behind them, coupled with the learning experiences from *Tornado*, it can be seen that the team behind the construction of No. 2007 stand every chance of delivering their

second project on or around the projected completion date of 2021. Given that, by that date, there will be only a tiny proportion of people who will be able to remember the original machines, most of us will be

experiencing something entirely new. With the design developed and finely honed to suit the world of 21st-century mainline steam, Gresley's mighty Mikado class P2 should be an enigma no more.

ABOVE: The face of a 21st-century P2, as seen in Darlington Locomotive Works in October 2016. A1SLT

RIGHT: Routine maintenance being carried out on the then-new P2 No. 2001 *Cock o' the North*.

Get on board now!

ABOVE: Jonathan Clay's painting of P2 No. 2007 *Prince of Wales*. A1SLT

The initial fundraising initiative in building No. 2007 *Prince of Wales* was The Founders' Club. A preliminary target of at least £100,000 from 100 'Founders' was set, but due to the overwhelming generosity of supporters, The A1 Steam Locomotive Trust raised more than £450,000 from in excess of 370 donors (see page 110).

Just as with *Tornado*, funds will be raised through regular monthly donations, which will be dedicated to specific components, various clubs and commercial sponsorship.

Why not become a covenantor – a P2 for the price of a pint!

Around 800 covenantors have already signed up worth around £1.5 million to the project. Covenantors donate £10 per month, but Gift Aid makes this worth £12.50.

The trust has set itself a target of 2000 covenantors.

In recognition of the covenantors' support, they will receive an opportunity to buy a ticket on one of No. 2007's first main line tours, have reasonable access to the build, a print of the launch painting of *Prince of Wales* by Jonathan Clay, monthly newsletters, invitations to various events, an opportunity to take part in an awards scheme and their name included on the Roll of Honour at Darlington Locomotive Works.

Currently, there are two clubs open, The Boiler Club and The Mikado Club.

The aim for The Boiler Club is to raise at least £600,000 from 300 supporters each donating £2000 in up to 40 payments of £50 – the trust is already more than one-third of the way there.

If the project to complete No. 2007 *Prince of Wales* in 2021 is to remain on schedule, the trust needs to wheel the engine by spring 2017 – hence the launch of The Mikado Club – 160 supporters each donating £1000 each (plus Gift Aid) to the project in up to eight payments of £125 by standing order.

There is also a unique opportunity for supporters to be associated with a component of No. 2007 and the funds raised will help to ensure the build remains on schedule.

Just as with *Tornado*, supporters will have the satisfaction of pointing to the part they paid for when No. 2007 enters service.

Dedicated donations range in price from one of more than 1000 driven bolts and nuts for £25 to the complete exhaust injector for £15,000 – an ideal present for the railway enthusiast in your family or just something for yourself, to show your support.

• For more information on how you can support the build of *Prince of Wales* please visit www.p2steam.com, call 01325 460163 or email enquiries@p2steam.com

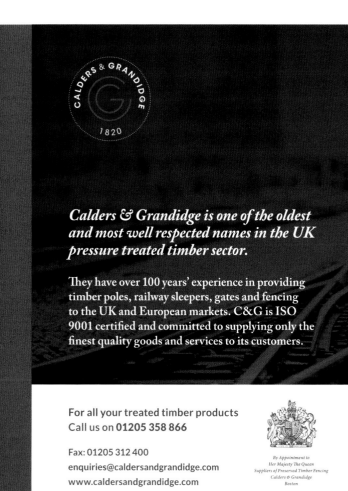

Chapter 13

Flying Scotsman opens Britain's newest station

The final big event of its comeback year saw *Flying Scotsman* return to where it all began – the East Lancashire Railway. Only this time round, for the *Scotsman* in Steam event on October 13-16, 2016, the A3 was painted in the correct Brunswick green, not in black as was the case during its first test runs on the heritage line back in January that year.

ABOVE: *Flying Scotsman* shimmers in the last rays of the sun while approaching Rawtenstall on the East Lancashire Railway on October 14. PETER AINSWORTH

More than 8500 people rode behind *Flying Scotsman* when it made its return visit to the East Lancashire Railway, nine months after it first ventured out of Ian Riley's Baron Street workshops in Bury for its inaugural test run.

Another 3500 people were said to have viewed it from a station on the heritage line during the October 13-16 *Scotsman* in Steam event, which also saw tickets snapped up briskly months in advance.

This time, the A3 did not carry the wartime black livery left over from its false restart in 2011, but Brunswick green, the correct livery for its latter-day British Railways guise.

Back on the line, its first duty was to help open the newest station in the heritage sector.

On Thursday, October 13, the locomotive headed a VIP special which departed the East Lancashire Railway's Bury (Bolton Street) station for the line's new Burrs Country Park halt. The Bolton Caledonian Pipe Band piped in No. 60103 with Scotland the Brave as it steamed up to a red ribbon. The A3 did not break the ribbon, but stopped short so it could just be dropped, and then it drew forward two coach lengths to allow the dignitaries to disembark.

There, the Mayor of Bury, Coun Mike Connolly, officially opened the station, the seventh on the heritage line alongside special guest Annabelle Griffin from Annabelle's Challenge, a Bury-based charity that had been set up in 2013 to raise awareness of vascular EDS, a rare genetic condition, to support medics, patients and their families.

The mayor spoke about what the new station means for both the railway and the locality.

The country park currently attracts more than 350,000 visitors each year and this figure is expected to increase following the opening of the new station, which is the centrepiece of a Bury Council development strategy that aims to establish Burrs as a 'destination park'. Under the long-term scheme, the country park will become a key element of Bury's tourism portfolio and a regional attraction, and the new station will support this vision by encouraging a new set of visitors to explore the park and its array of attractions, including the Irwell Sculpture Trail, Activity Centre and Caravan Club site. That site currently has 80 pitches, but now the new station has been opened, the number of pitches will increase by 25%.

East Lancashire Railway chairman Mike Kelly said: "Today has been a momentous day for the ELR, as not only have we welcomed

Flying Scotsman back to our line for the second time this year but we have officially opened a brand new station at Burrs Country Park. The community is really at the heart of the new station, thus it is fitting that *Flying Scotsman* – "The People's Engine" – was the first locomotive to call at the stop.

"The railway has worked with local residents, businesses and societies on the station's development strategy over the past few years and hopes that the community will find the new station an exciting and beneficial addition."

The new station project next to the River Irwell a mile north of Bury town centre has been managed by Bury-based builder Cheetham Hill Construction, whose representatives were also on the VIP special, as were pupils from Woodbank Primary School, the nearest school to Burrs Country Park, who displayed a project on *Flying Scotsman* and the new station.

After the opening, the train continued on its return trip to Rawtenstall.

The *Scotsman* in Steam event included luxury dining trains and a lineside photography course.

The station will open to the public from January 2017 and will enable visitors to the country park to board heritage services to

ABOVE: *Flying Scotsman* hauled a special dining train over the line on October 14. It is seen at Bury (Bolton Street) station. The photographer is Liam Barnes, a 15-year-old rail and photography enthusiast from Bury, who aims to become a member of the railway when he reaches 16. LIAM BARNES

Heywood, Bury, Summerseat, Ramsbottom, Irwell Vale and Rawtenstall.

It is the latest development in the 30-year success story of what has become, like the Severn Valley and North Yorkshire Moors railways, an established member of the Premier League of UK heritage lines.

British Rail withdrew passenger services between Bury and Rawtenstall on June 3, 1972. Coal services to Rawtenstall ended in 1980, and formal closure followed in 1982. The route from Bury to Manchester was subsequently converted into an arm of the city's Metrolink light rail network.

However, the line which runs through the scenic Irwell Valley quickly came to the attention of revivalists, and the East Lancashire

Railway Trust reopened it in stages from July 25, 1987.

The first services operated between Bury (Bolton Street) and Ramsbottom. In 1991 the service was extended northwards from Ramsbottom to Rawtenstall, which became the line's northern terminus.

In September 2003, the line eastern 'branch' extension from Bury to Heywood was reopened. To reach Heywood, the extension had to cross over the Metrolink line to Bury, at the site of the former Bury (Knowsley Street) station. This necessitated the construction of a new intersection bridge, with steeply graded approaches of 1-in-36 and 1-in-41 nicknamed 'the Ski Jump'.

The heritage line is now just over 12 miles

long, and has a main line connection at Castleton, to the east of Heywood. It is the third most popular paid visitor attraction in Greater Manchester and welcomes more than 160,000 visitors each year, making a major contribution to its local economy.

The railway is planning to extend services to Castleton, to a new and separate platform named Castleton Village, adjacent to the main line station. Plans for the new station are supported by Rochdale Borough Council, which hopes to fund it by adjacent land development.

A rail connection with the Metrolink line also exists, just south of Bury, at Buckley Wells, and on rare occasions, heritage shunters diesel and steam have been hired to haul night-time maintenance and works trains.

ABOVE: *Flying Scotsman* at Bury on September 28, 2016 after arriving from its exploits on the Severn Valley Railway. ELR

ABOVE: The A3 is welcomed to the sound of Scotland the Brave. PAUL BICKERDYKE

ABOVE: No. 60103 stops short of the ceremonial ribbon. PAUL BICKERDYKE

ABOVE: The commemorative plaque to mark the station opening with *Flying Scotsman*. PAUL BICKERDYKE

RIGHT: The VIP party at the opening of Burrs Country Park station, from left to right: Ian Hargreaves (Mayor of Bury's consort), Annabelle Griffin (Annabelle's Challenge), Coun Mike Connolly (Mayor of Bury), Coun Rishi Shori (leader of Bury Council) and Mike Kelly (chairman of the East Lancashire Railway). Annabelle, six, was invited along as the mayor's guest. In December 2012, she was diagnosed with Vascular Ehlers-Danlos Syndrome, a very rare medical condition, which is life threatening and incurable, and a charity has been set up to promote treatment and research, with it helping to host a major conference in Manchester next year. More details are available at www.annabelleschallenge.org RORY LUSHMAN/ELR

BELOW: *Flying Scotsman* pulls into Burrs Country Park halt on October 16, 2016. PAUL BICKERDYKE

£6.8 million – was it worth it?

In October 2016, the National Railway Museum announced the full and final cost of saving *Flying Scotsman* for the nation and returning this iconic steam legend to the tracks.

Revising the previous figure for the cost of its overhaul by £300,000 to £4,537,892 – over and above the initial purchase price of £2.31 million – officials pointed out that since its high-profile return earlier this year, more than 200,000 people will have seen the locomotive at the museum's York and Shildon sites and at heritage railway events – and millions more worldwide watching it on their TV screens.

The revision of the overhaul cost was attributed to the final stages of the restoration revealing that more remedial work than anticipated was needed to some parts of the locomotive that had been thought fit for purpose, coupled with a tight deadline to meet the inaugural run date in February 2016. Over the decade that the overhaul had dragged on, there were critics seemingly at every corner. Why did the museum have to buy it in the first place when a prospective private owner was prepared to bid? Why not leave it simply as a static museum exhibit? Bearing in mind that an A1 Pacific costs £3 million to build from new, with hindsight, the cost of the purchase and overhaul of No. 4472 would have paid for two A3s – and one could have included all the surviving original parts from *Flying Scotsman*, thereby giving it the right to call itself the real McCoy.

However, such criticisms seem to have dissipated like a will o' the wisp since the big green machine began strutting its stuff across the country.

Museum director Paul Kirkman said: "Saving *Scotsman* for the nation has been a complex project but eminently worthwhile. Since its return this year, the spectacular sight of this most famous of steam locomotives has captured the imagination and been a life-enhancing experience for thousands, possibly millions of people.

"As well as those who have seen it in action on the tracks on rail tours and appearing at heritage railway events across the UK, visitors

Bricking it with *Flying Scotsman*

FLYING Scotsman in green livery had already wowed the crowds in the North West in the summer of 2016.

An eight-metre-long model of the A3 and three carriages formed the centrepiece of a LEGO exhibition at Rheged, the Lakeland heritage centre sited in a former quarry near Penrith, with a huge 3D cinema screen.

The exhibition – Bricks in Time: Hands on History in LEGO – was curated by Bright Bricks, the only professional modelmakers in the UK to be endorsed by the Danish toy company.

The 1-in-10 scale model locomotive, which is 40cm high and 30cm wide, took more than 550 hours to build from around 100,000 individual pieces. If bought in the shops, the bricks could cost up to £10,000.

The locomotive itself is 2.2 metres long, and stands at the front of a train comprising cut-away illuminated carriages in the form of a sleeping car, a dining car and a lounge car, all populated with LEGO people.

The model was displayed alongside a sound machine with recordings of the real *Flying Scotsman* and a smoke machine.

Ed Diment from Bright Bricks said: "We've worked on LEGO projects of all shapes and sizes over the years. This new model of the *Flying Scotsman* is

quite possibly the loveliest thing we've ever made from LEGO. We've used the inside of the carriages to tell a story and imagine what life was like when the train was first in service."

Although the firm has no current confirmed plans for taking its *Flying Scotsman* on tour, its shows, including the A3, can be hired for events. BRIGHT BRICKS

to our museums have been able to get up close and experience the most famous locomotive and express train service in the world first-hand, through our free innovative exhibitions and displays. This globetrotting screen star and multiple record-breaker will continue to be seen around the UK, demonstrating the engineering science behind steam traction to new generations of fans."

Former cabinet minister Michael Portillo, travelling on the train as part of filming for BBC documentary series Great British Railway Journeys, described *Flying Scotsman* as an "engineering triumph", adding: "This is certainly the most famous journey and most famous locomotive in Britain."

As we saw earlier, it has been said that many youngsters who were taken by their parents to see *Flying Scotsman* may never have seen a working steam locomotive before. And ask traders in Kidderminster, Bridgnorth, Bury and Pickering and those in the towns that No. 60103 will visit in the years ahead whether the money spent was worth it. Yes – mistakes were made, but the nation now has a treasure back that it has always been proud of, and always will be.

The comeback has also done much to raise the public profile of the railway heritage sector, which is a major player in the UK tourist market, and may well increase its share, if more people decide to take holidays at home in

view of the falling pound on the foreign current markets in the Brexit era.

The restoration was financed with the help of a Heritage Lottery Fund grant of £275,000. The aim of the purchase had always been to operate *Flying Scotsman* as a working museum exhibit and ambassador for the work of the museum to preserve Britain's rich railway heritage for the nation, showcasing its impact, past, present and future.

After its jaunt on the East Lancashire Railway, *Flying Scotsman* returned home to the York museum for its winter maintenance, and visitors over the ensuing Christmas holidays were set to see the star locomotive on its home turf. ●

BELOW: *Flying Scotsman* heads an East Lancashire Railway service through the Irwell valley on October 14. LIAM BARNES

Chapter 14

Remembering the *Scotsman* season

The belated return of *Flying Scotsman* to Britain's rails in 2016 has gripped the public imagination and has added to the legend that is the world's most famous steam locomotive.

Proud owner, the National Railway Museum, has produced an unprecedented amount of souvenirs to suit all ages and pockets to celebrate the comeback year, and here are just a few.

All of these products and many more are currently available in the National Railway Museum shops at York and at Locomotion in Shildon. Alternatively they can be ordered online at www.nrmshop.co.uk or via mail order on 0844 815 3139. Postage and packing is £5.99 for UK delivery, more for Europe.

ABOVE: *Flying Scotsman* Returns to York Station in 2016 mounted print, £12.

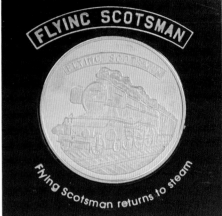

ABOVE: *Flying Scotsman* commemorative coin, £10.

BELOW: *Flying Scotsman* teddy bear, £10.

RIGHT: *Flying Scotsman* weekend bag, £85.

BELOW: *Flying Scotsman* tin with toffees, £14.

ABOVE: *Flying Scotsman* commemorative medallion, £20.

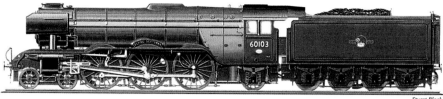

A3 Class 4-6-2   **ABOVE:** *Flying Scotsman* side view print by Stuart Black, £5.

Stuart Black

60103 Flying Scotsman

ABOVE: Green *Flying Scotsman* nameplate T-shirt various sizes, £15.

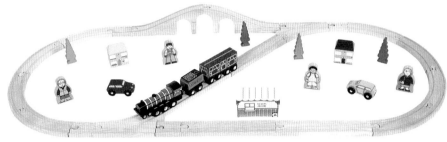

ABOVE: Bigjigs Brio-style wooden push-along *Flying Scotsman* train set, £35.

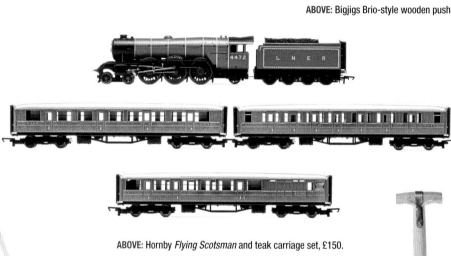

ABOVE: *Flying Scotsman* 3D brass nameplate, £100.

ABOVE: Hornby *Flying Scotsman* and teak carriage set, £150.

RIGHT: *Flying Scotsman* replica coal shovel, £100.

ABOVE: Metal *Flying Scotsman* bookmark, £8.

RIGHT: A pair of *Flying Scotsman* socks, £8.

BELOW: *Flying Scotsman* postcard pack, £8.

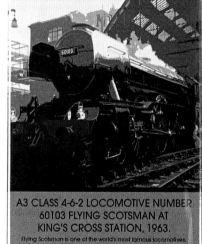

A3 CLASS 4-6-2 LOCOMOTIVE NUMBER 60103 FLYING SCOTSMAN AT KING'S CROSS STATION, 1963.

Flying Scotsman is one of the world's most famous locomotives. It was built in 1923, by the London & North Eastern Railway's Doncaster works. In 1928, Flying Scotsman completed its first non stop run from London to Edinburgh. The journey was 393 miles; at that time, the longest journey in the world. In 1934, Flying Scotsman became the first steam locomotive to achieve an authenticated speed of 100mph.

ABOVE: *Flying Scotsman* at King's Cross in 1963 fridge magnet, £2.50.

BELOW: Brio-style Bigjigs version of *Flying Scotsman*, £14.

ABOVE: Flatpack metal *Flying Scotsman* model kit, £8.

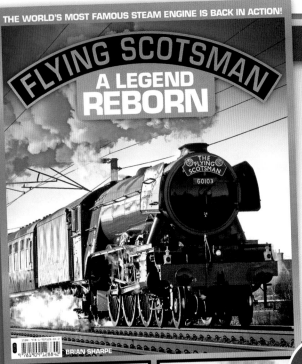

Chapter 15

And for the next ones...

Even before the building of *Tornado* had reached the halfway stage, it was an open secret that The A1 Steam Locomotive Trust aimed to follow it up by building a Gresley P2. Similarly, with the *Prince of Wales* project having become the fastest-growing new-build project of all time, the trust has announced what will be its next projects.

ABOVE: V4 No. 1700 *Bantam Cock* heads a Down freight on the West Highland Line at Ardlui in August 1948. BEN BROOKSBANK

Apart from the announcement that *Tornado* was to undergo 90mph test running in early 2017 and have its own rake of modern coaches assembled, supporters at The A1 Steam Locomotive Trust's annual convention in Darlington on October 1, 2016, were not only told about what would be the group's next new-build project – but the one after that too.

In April 2014, the trust announced that it was hoping to plug one of three gaps in the UK heritage fleet by building a new example of one of Gresley's smaller locomotive types, which had also been rendered extinct before the end of British Railways steam.

It must be remembered that the LNER fared badly in the preservation stakes at the end of steam, when compared to the other three 'Big Four' companies' locomotives. Barry scrapyard proprietor Dai Woodham, who bought hundreds of redundant steam locomotives from British Railways for scrap, made a momentous decision to "save them for a rainy day" before scrapping them, and instead concentrate on the more lucrative business of cutting up wagons. Thanks to him, a total of 213 steam locomotives were saved for preservation use – but only one of them was an LNER type, B1 4-6-0 No. 61264. The others that were saved came predominantly from the GWR and Southern Railway, which were much closer to Barry.

LNER and LMS locomotives also went to local scrapyards, but ones which dismantled them within days, rendering many classes extinct at a stroke.

Back in 2014, the trust had drawn up a shortlist of three Gresley locomotive types as its next project, the K3 2-6-0, the V3 suburban 2-6-2T and the V4 2-6-2.

The list has now been narrowed down to a V4 first, followed by a V3.

Gresley's mixed traffic three-cylinder V4s comprised his final design before he died in 1941, and had similarities both in their appearance and mechanical layout to the V2s.

Indeed, the V4s were seen as a lightweight alternative to the V2s, and unlike the Green Arrow class which had limited route availability, could be used all over the whole of the LNER network.

Two locomotives were built at Doncaster in 1941, No. 3401 *Bantam Cock*, which had a scaled-down version of Gresley Pacific's boiler, and No. 3402, nicknamed Bantam Hen, with a fully welded steel firebox. These comprised the entire class. The V4s had similarities in their appearance and mechanical layout to the earlier V2 2-6-2s, of which No. 4771 *Green Arrow* is the sole survivor. The V4 was a lightweight alternative, suitable for use over the whole of the LNER network.

The pair were well received during trials on the Great Eastern section of the LNER, where they were well liked, showing more

power than the existing B17s and with better riding qualities.

However, a production batch was never built. After Gresley's death, his successor Edward Thompson built no more, and instead his B1 4-6-0 became the LNER's standard mixed-traffic locomotive.

The two locomotives were reallocated to the West Highland Line, but their wheel arrangement was not particularly suitable for the steep gradients. Renumbered 1700 and 1701 in 1946, they became BR Nos. 61700 and 61701. Both were scrapped in 1957 when their boilers became due for renewal.

It is intended by the trust that the new V4 will become the third member of the class, rather than a replica of the earlier two. Work will be starting within the next 12 months on a design book to be created within 3D CAD.

A new Gresley tank

ABOVE: Gresley V3 2-6-2T No. 390 at Doncaster in 1939. A1SLT

The V3 was a development of Gresley's earlier V1 2-6-2T with increased boiler pressure and a resultant increase in tractive effort.

A total of 82 V1s were built with 71 being rebuilt into the higher pressure V3s with an additional 10 being built as V3s from the final batch of V1s.

The design has its roots in the Sevenoaks derailment of August 24, 1927, in which 13 people died. It was thought that a primary factor in the disaster was the instability of Maunsell's large K or River class 2-6-4Ts – No. 800 *River Cray* had been pulling the train, but Gresley carried out stability tests on one of these locomotives and found no problem with it.

He then proceeded to produce his V1 suburban tank which appeared three years later. It incorporated his three-cylinder system: it was the first example of all three cylinders and valve chests being incorporated into a single steel casting.

The same arrangement was used for the first P2, No. 2001 *Cock o' the North*, and the subsequent V2, K4 and V4 classes.

ABOVE: The first of the two V4s, No. 3401 *Bantam Cock*, at Doncaster in 1941. A1SLT

The V3s were first used in Scotland on the Glasgow-Edinburgh-Helensburgh services, and many were later used on the Newcastle-Middlesbrough route. Several of them also saw service on suburban and branch line workings in Hull.

V1s and V3s were later superseded first by Edward Thompson's more powerful L1 class, and then DMUs. Withdrawals began in 1960, with the last V1 scrapped by 1962 and the last V3 by 1964, the class having been displaced by DMUs.

Trust chairman Mark Allatt said that it was ironic that the LNER, which placed importance on railway heritage, opening the original railway museum in York, did so badly in terms of locomotive preservation, leaving many such gaps to be filled. "While GWR, Southern and BR Standard followers did so well out of Barry, only one engine, B1 No. 61264, was saved from there," he said.

"Apart from D49 No. 246 *Morayshire*, none of the smaller Gresley original designs survive. The N2 tank (the Gresley Trust owns the sole survivor, No. 1744) is just an improved version of an earlier design." ●

ABOVE: Was this the last picture taken of *Bantam Cock*? The locomotive is already stripped of its nameplates and coupling rods, and appears to be awaiting the scrapman. A1SLT

BELOW: V3 2-6-2T No. 67628 at an undisclosed location. A1SLT